THE MATHESON MONOGRAPHS

The principal objective of the Matheson Trust is to promote the study of comparative religion from the point of view of the underlying harmony of the great religious and philosophical traditions of the world. This objective is being pursued through such means as audio-visual media, the support and sponsorship of lecture series and conferences, the creation of a website, collaboration with film production companies and publishing companies as well as the Trust's own series of publications.

The Matheson Monographs will cover a wide range of themes within the field of comparative religion: scriptural exegesis in different religious traditions; the modalities of spiritual and contemplative life; in-depth mystical studies of particular religious traditions; broad comparative analyses taking in a series of religious forms; studies of traditional arts, crafts and cosmological sciences; and contemporary scholarly expositions of religious philosophy and metaphysics. The monographs will also comprise translations of both classical and contemporary texts as well as transcriptions of lectures by, and interviews with, spiritual and scholarly authorities from different religious and philosophical traditions.

HERMES TRISMEGISTUS

Ἡσύχασον, ὦ τέκνον, καὶ τῆς ἁρμοζούσης νῦν ἄκουε εὐλογίας, τὸν ὕμνον τῆς παλιγγενεσίας... τοῦτο οὐ διδάσκεται, ἀλλὰ κρύπτεται ἐν σιγῇ... ἡσύχασον, ὦ τέκνον.

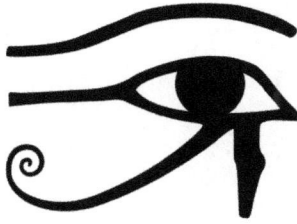

Be still, O son, hear the harmonious song of praise, the hymn of rebirth... This hymn is not taught but hid in silence... Be still, O son.
(*Corpus Hermeticum* XIII. 16)

HERMES TRISMEGISTUS
THE WAY OF WISDOM

by Algis Uždavinys

Translated from Lithuanian by
Rūta Rimkienė

THE MATHESON TRUST
For the Study of Comparative Religion

First published as:
Hermio Trismegisto išminties kelias
Vilnius: Sophia, 2005.

This translation © The Matheson Trust, 2025

This first English edition published 2025 by
The Matheson Trust
31 Hayne Rd, Beckenham
Kent BR3 4JA, United Kingdom
http://themathesontrust.org

ISBN: 978 1 908092 25 0

British Library Cataloguing-in-Publication Data.
A catalogue record for this book is
available from the British Library

Cover design and typesetting by Susana Marín.

CONTENTS

CHAPTER 1: THE ARCHETYPAL AND HISTORICAL FORMS
OF HERMES TRISMEGISTUS

CHAPTER 2: THE EGYPTIAN GOD THOTH AND THE
HERMETIC TRADITION

CHAPTER 3: HERMETIC PHILOSOPHY AND INITIATION

ABBREVIATIONS

DH: *Définitions d'Hermès Trismégiste à Asclépius*
Ascl.: *Asclepius*
CH: *Corpus Hermeticum*
SH: *Stobaei Hermetica*
NHC: *Coptic codices of Nag Hammadi*
PT: Pyramid Texts

EDITOR'S PREFACE

This is the second posthumous publication by our dear friend and colleague Algis Uždavinys, and the first one to be translated by his own daughter from a Lithuanian original. After a long and laborious editorial process, I feel that some introductory words may prove useful, especially for readers new to his works.

One must read Algis with intent, conscious that here was not an author to waste time on pleasantries, on paying lip-service to any institutions or flaunting school allegiances of any kind. He was where he was, by the grace of God and for Truth, and he wrote from that very same stance, uncompromising. In few other authors do we find such a total devotion to the famous medieval maxim, *Amicus Plato sed magis amica veritas* ("I love Plato, but I love Truth even more"). For readers, this attitude is both a rare gift and an intimate pressing call to relinquish trite reasonings and comfortable "intellectual" standpoints, and to confront the bare Truth again and again, trusting Algis as an inspired guide.

Reading Algis with attention means in turn coming face to face, walking side by side, or sheltering under the wing of an intellectual giant and a profoundly contemplative mind. Along the way, and particularly in this book, three moments are discernible: first is the awareness that there is no end of things to know—that is, marvelling at *scientia*, *episteme*, the endlessness of creation. Second, there is the clear understanding that there is a restricted number of things we *really* need to know—the "one thing needful". Finally, as the Hermetic learning is accomplished, there is the realisation that there is no end of things to know—the infinity of being.

And under the student's eyes the cosmic forms now unfold in stellated patterns, now merge towards an ever-receding and ever-desirable crystallisation, the ultimate Love of philosophers. These three moments naturally reflect the essence of this book, because Hermes is the divine mediator between the sciences of created beings and the gnosis of uncreated realities—and this is not just a book about Hermes but also a Hermetic book.

As with some of his other works, it feels as if this monograph, written well before the author's death, is under the spell of the Sufi saying, "Time is like a sword: if you don't cut it, it cuts you" (*al-waqt ka'l-sayf in lam taqta'hu qata'ak*). With every page it is as if Algis is saying, "Reader, there is no time to lose, and you know what to do." We hope that our readers will be able to benefit from this urgent appeal, to avail themselves through these pages of Algis Uždavinys' congenial and rigorous friendship.

On a typographical note, we have preferred—like Algis in his late works—to leave Greek terms in transliteration, thus maintaining a certain continuity with his previous publications in English.

Juan Acevedo
Lisbon, August 2024

PREFACE

The philosophical and alchemical texts purportedly written by the mythical Hermes Trismegistus and his followers are regarded as harbingers of divine knowledge. They belong to the Hermetic tradition, which thrived in Egypt back in the days of Hellenism and the Roman Empire. The entity these texts address as *Hermes* is actually Thoth, the Egyptian god of wisdom, writing, magic and science, who also possesses a myriad of metaphysical and iconographic aspects. The Hermeticism of Late Antiquity is the result of the synthesis between the Egyptian and the Hellenic tradition.

Despite the secluded and esoteric nature of the Hermetic fraternities, some of their texts reached Western Europe and played an essential role in shaping the worldview of the Renaissance. The transformed post-Renaissance Hermeticism (which was directed against the dominant Christian mythology and Aristotelianism) laid the foundation for modern, experimental science. Despite this, Hermeticism is a foreign concept to the contemporary person, unless they specialise in ancient history or esotericism. The fault lies in the official Western historiography (both Christian and secular, not necessarily positivistic), which deliberately obscures or alters certain episodes of the past that might not align well with its "promotional image".

The aim of this research monograph is to reveal the attributes of Hermetic philosophy and practice by discussing the problematic question of the origin of Hermeticism and its historical spread. By analysing the worldview and religious iconography of the ancient Egyptians, the transformations of Hellenic culture, and various aspects of theurgy and magic, we attempt to demonstrate that the tradition of Hermes

Trismegistus' wisdom, which is both multifarious and homogeneous, can be genetically traced back to the sacred
teachings of Ancient Egypt in spite of being conveyed in
Hellenistic philosophical terms. By focusing on the acceptance of Hermetic ideas in the Islamic world (especially in the
periods of the Umayyads and Abbasids) and Renaissance
Europe (from the late fifteenth century), we will demonstrate
the various fantastical transformations that doctrines related
to Hermes underwent, how they function in the context of
mythical genealogies, and how they shape the scope of cultural identity with the help of imagination.

When discussing the ever-changing variety of Hermetic
tropes and mythologems, it is easy to lose oneself in a sea
of heterogeneous information. For this reason, we will discuss only a part of the Hermetic tradition in order to reveal
its metaphysical connection to the Ancient Egyptian wisdom
texts, as well as the peripeteia of historical dispersion, which
has little to do with the original source.

In the first chapter of this monograph, we explore the
many faces of Thoth-Hermes—his depiction, appraisal and
propagation in the worlds of Islam and Christianity. We also
discuss how the mythical image of Hermes functioned in different cultural contexts, becoming an almost magical-cosmo-
logical emblem, which served specific political, social, scientific, philosophical, artistic, and occult purposes.

The second chapter attempts to reveal the religious-philosophical meaning behind the iconography of Thoth and
other gods associated with him. This lets us see the specific
connections between the ancient Egyptian and Hellenic cultures, allowing for an exploration of their multifaceted and
complicated symbiosis.

In the third chapter we talk about Hermeticism from the
perspective of religious and cultic practices such as the doctrine of rebirth, as well as the methods of spiritual ascension
and alchemical transformations, which should not be artificially detached from the purely "philosophical" Hermeticism.

CHAPTER 1

THE ARCHETYPAL AND HISTORICAL
FORMS OF HERMES TRISMEGISTUS

Thoth (Eg. *dhwty*) is the ancient Egyptian god of wisdom, referred to as Hermes Trismegistus in the era of Ptolemaic Egypt. His multifaceted image merged with the image of Hermes (the messenger of the Olympian gods described by Homer) in the imagination of the Hellenic people at the times of Assyria and the early Persian Achaemenid Empire. On the one hand, Thoth-Hermes is perceived as a divine archetype, a complex of metaphysical prototypes and theophanies. On the other hand, his name is used to declare, legitimise and maintain various philosophical, cosmological, grammatological, liturgical and magical traditions. It is difficult to make sense of this abundance of philosophical categories, literary fantasies, cultic-iconographic forms and mythical images. Divine knowledge might easily turn into an "encyclopedia of nonsense", while seemingly naive and absurd symbols (from the perspective of the discursive mind) might reveal the most mysterious depths of being.

In spite of their empirical and experimental nature, Hermetic sciences are based on the power of intellectual imagination. Many ancient arts and sciences rely on the authority of the scribe of the gods. In a cosmological sense, Thoth-Hermes is equivalent to *Logos*, the "Word" that formed the universe. His name is associated with the spiritual path that leads to perfection and divine integrity or, more precisely, to

1

various methods of philosophical purification, alchemical transformation and theurgical ascent, which were varyingly adapted by most Mediterranean and Middle Eastern cultic and philosophical communities, especially at the time of syncretic Hellenism.

If we consider the concept of "archetypal authorship", whereby a renowned historical or mythical hero (such as Orpheus, Solomon, or Aristotle) is used as a "front" for entire traditions, genres, and philosophical trends, it is unsurprising that Hermes Trismegistus is credited as the author of countless literary works, both lost and preserved. Some researchers—especially those who tend to project rationalistic classification systems onto the past—attempt to divide Hermetic literature into two contrasting categories by adopting the modernist antithesis of "rationality" versus "superstition", thus painting an inadequate picture of the past. This insistence on differentiating between "high" and "low" Hermeticism can lead to a shallow misunderstanding—a schematic and presumptive interpretation, which merely reflects the viewpoint of modern researchers rather than the original followers of Hermes. In regard to terminology, it might be more reasonable to divide Hermeticism into "philosophical" and "technical", however, even this kind of division remains questionable.

First, we need to determine the exact meaning behind the words "philosophical Hermetica". In short, the philosophical Hermetica consist of Egyptian philosophical dialogues and collections of texts (written between the third century BC and the fourth century AD) that reinterpret Thoth's wisdom teachings using the terminology of Middle Platonism and Stoicism. According to the followers of Hermes, these are the translations of hieroglyphic texts (or the doctrines that they convey), which were adapted for Hellenic philosophical discourse and for an altered cultural environment. (Some modern researchers categorically deny this version, referring to Hermetic teachings as marginal Platonism). Unfortunately, the original texts, written by Hermeticists from Ptolemaic and Roman Egypt, survived only in fragments, some of which were later edited and censored by Christian authors. Nevertheless, these texts are what we call Hermes Trismegistus' wisdom texts, or *philosophical Hermetica*. However, as is correctly noted by G. Fowden, the categories of "technical", "philosophical" and "spiritual" do not align with the Hermetic way of thinking[1] and represent the ideas of the nineteenth-century Europe's Positivistic-Romanticist environment rather than the ideas of Late Antiquity. The images of Hermes as a philosopher and Hermes as a master of practical arts are often merged. It is possible that Byzantine Christians cleansed the "philosophical Hermetica" of everything that appeared strongly related to "pagan" ritual practices.

In addition, it is important to note that, in a collection of Hermetic texts in Russian, edited by K. Boguckis, even an excerpt from the *Pyramid Texts* is classified as "low" Hermeticism.[2] This obscures the definition of "Hermeticism"—does it encompass everything related (or seemingly related) to the names of the Egyptian god Thoth and the cultural hero Hermes Trismegistus, or only the teachings of certain elite Roman communities? On the contrary, what researchers refer to as "technical" Hermetica are magical, alchemical and astrological texts, based on the authority of Hermes or directly attributed to Thoth-Hermes and other related characters. However, the alchemists who follow Hermes Trismegistus also call their craft (*techne*) philosophy. In terms of Antiquity, the act of "philosophising" is not limited to the dialectical thinkers of the Academy—it is also done by dervish-like Cynics, scribes of Egyptian temples, enthusiasts of Pythagorean ascesis, Chaldeans and even Indian Gymnosophists.[3]

For now, let's leave Arabic texts behind and confine ourselves to the narrow context of Christian Europe which will let

---

1. Garth Fowden, *The Egyptian Hermes. A Historical Approach to the Late Pagan Mind*, Princeton University Press, Princeton, 1993, p. 89.

2. Гермес Трисмегист и герметическая традиция Востока и Запада, tr. by К.Богуцкий, Iris, Kiev; Алетейа, Moscow, 1998.

3. Algis Uždavinys, *Vėlyvosios antikos filosofijos bruožai*. Logos, 2000, N.23, pp. 6-23.

us define the contours of philosophical Hermetica rather easily. The collection of texts, attributed to Hermes Trismegistus
and his students, is comprised of:

1. *Corpus Hermeticum* that consists of sixteen books (Lat
   libelli) with excerpts from Hermetical dialogues in
   Greek. The number of the treatises goes up to eighteen,
   but the fifteenth is missing, and the eighteenth was add
   ed later. For a long time, this collection was referred to
   by the name of the first book (*Libellus I*), *Hermou tris-
   megistou Poimandres*, or *Mercurii Trismegisti Poemander*.
2. *Asclepius: The Perfect Discourse of Hermes Trismegistus*
   (*Logos teleios; Sermo perfectus*)—a translation of a dialogue
   from Greek to Latin, once mistakenly attributed to
   Apuleius, a Platonist philosopher. The original text did
   not survive.
3. Twenty-seven excerpts from an anthology compiled by a
   Byzantian author named Stobaeus (circa 500 AD).
4. A number of quotes from Hellenic and Christian authors.

Thus, this is the list "canonized" by the adepts of classical
philosophy. However, it could be greatly extended if all the
works related to sacred rituals, alchemy, astrology, medicine,
mathematics, occult botany and talismanic science were classified as "philosophy", or the "high" category of Hermeticism—
especially those mentioned in Arabic sources or fragments of
Egyptian papyri.

As there is a lot of confusion regarding definitions, English-
speaking researchers sometimes refer to teachings of philosophical Hermetica (which are similar to Middle Platonism)
as "Hermetism". However, when defining a wider scope of
Hermetic legacy, its texts and doctrines (usually alchemical
and astrological), these teachings are called "Hermeticism".
The term "hermetic", which means airtight or sealed, is common in scientific and everyday vocabulary. However, it is
merely a banal reflection of allusions to the secret teachings
of Hermes. Hermeneutics, as a practice of interpretation and

a methodology of revealing a hidden meaning, is also related to the name of Hermes, the hermeneut of gods, even though certain pedantic etymologists (J. Grondin could be considered one of them) do not see a direct genetic link between these words.

When we speak about Thoth-Hermes of Antiquity, as well as real and imaginary Hermetic traditions, we have to emphasise that syncretic Hermeticism (i.e. a combination of the Jewish Kabbalah, Biblical stories, etc.), which emerged and thrived in the environment of Western occultism (especially during the Renaissance), has little to do with the authentic tradition of ancient Egypt, and has almost nothing to do with the mythical theology of Egypt of the pharaonic era. In other words, degraded Egyptian magic reached Middle Age and Renaissance Europe in the form of barely recognisable remains and rumours. U. Eco wrote:

> As a civilization, Egypt no longer existed, and for the Europeans it was not yet a land for future conquest. Ignored in its geopolitical inconsistency, it became a Hermetical phantom. In this role it could be identified as the spiritual ancestor of the Christian West, the progenitor of the occident's patrimony of mystic wisdom.[4]

According to S. H. Nasr, "one of the important results of the contact between the Egyptian and Greek traditions in Alexandria was the emergence of a particular school of wisdom known as Hermeticism."[5] We will attempt to analyse real and fictitious connections between Hermetic philosophy and Ancient Egypt. The statement that this "school of wisdom" emerged in Alexandria is a presumption of nineteenth-century historians. Earlier, it was popular to talk about a "school

---

4. Umberto Eco, *The Search for the Perfect Language*, Blackwell, Oxford, 1995, p.161.
5. Seyyed Hossein Nasr, *Hermes and Hermetic writings in the Islamic World*, SUNY Press, New York, 1981, p.102.

of Alexandria" as an amalgamation of different religious and philosophical currents. Recently, the role of Memphis, Panopolis, Hermopolis, Thebes and the cities of the Faiyum Oasis has become more apparent thanks to translations and reinterpretations of ancient Egyptian texts.

At the beginning of the twentieth century, there was an attempt to recreate a homogeneous synthetic image of Hermetic philosophy. However, most researchers have abandoned this Hegelian idea. Similar texts are simply classified into groups by concepts and style. This highlights different philosophical currents and tendencies. The label of Hermeticism, which unites these groups of texts, is often merely nominal. It is perceived either as a shared archetypal origin (from the perspective of every tradition based on the authority of Hermes) or as a symbolic axis, connecting the mosaic of religious-philosophical concepts.

To think that Hermetic tradition encompasses only a dual cosmological wisdom, meaning its macrocosmic and microcosmic aspects, as opposed to metaphysical wisdom (in agreement with R. Guénon, precursor of modern traditionalism),[6] means to give in to the hypnosis of classifications. This case illustrates the ideal twofold hierarchical structure of medieval Christianity, which has two dimensions: external (exoteric) and internal (esoteric). The internal is mystical monism, which yearns for connection with the divine (e.g. Eckhart's partly Neoplatonic version of Christianity). In this case, Hermeticism is merely a supplementary dimension of esoterism, a source of universal alchemical symbolism and the cornerstone of sacred arts and crafts, equivalent to "Lesser Mysteries". From a metaphysical point of view, it is a convenient system, reflecting the realities of both traditional Christian and Islamic civilisations.

However, when talking about the philosophical Hermeticism of Antiquity (represented by the doctrines of, for

---

6. René Guénon, *The Reign of Quantity and the Signs of the Times*, tr. by Lord Northbourne, Penguin Books, Baltimore, 1972.

example, *Poimandres* and *Asclepius*), we cannot really say that its spiritual and theurgic aspirations are different from the gnostic ideals of early Christianity. In the context of Late Antiquity, Hermeticism is "devalued" by the aggressive rhetoric of Christian monopoly, which strives for "orthodox" autocracy and regards all "pagan" wisdom traditions (Platonism included) as an information source at best, from which it can secretly borrow certain elements and present them as organic components of the Christian worldview.

In Medieval and Renaissance Europe, the Hermetic tradition operated under the Latin name of Mercury, which, in the field of material transformations, carried the meaning of a lively spirit or quicksilver. This tradition was indirectly formed by gathering small fragments of the science of Antiquity, translating random Arabic works by authors from the Islamic world, as well as integrating the teachings of Spanish Jews. This phantasmagoric fusion of symbols, emblems, cosmological images, magical recipes and astrological allegories constitutes a whole new version of European "Hermeticism". That is why it is important to differentiate between historical and mythological contexts, which cultivate various deviations of Hermetic tradition. From this extensive perspective, "Hermeticism" is equivalent to 1) the horizon of a correspondent way of thinking, divine experimental methodology (often directed against Aristotle's *Physics*) or 2) eclectic studies of arithmology, astrology, alchemy and magic (covered by an obscure label of Hermes-Mercury) in search of analogies, sympathetic connections and symbolic equivalents between the macrocosm and the human microcosm.

Therefore, it is not surprising that Hermes can be perceived as having an archetypal function, a mythical personification of certain paradigms. For this reason, the traditionalists of the *sophia perennis* school (who are also concerned with "comparative theology", which was already popular during the Hellenistic period) claim that "Hermes" is a single metaphysical entity, which manifests itself in different forms across various cultures. He is Hermes, the son of Zeus and Maia, Idris, an Arabian prophet (who, according to al-Biruni, is equivalent to Budhasaf, i.e. Maia's son Buddha), Jewish Enoch (*Henokh, Ukhnukh*), Persian Hushang or Gayomart, Germanic Odin (Votan) and even the winged Aztec serpent Quetzalcoatl. The above-mentioned traditionalists (R. Guénon, T. Burckhardt, S. H. Nasr) define *archetype* as a transcendent prototype, a Platonic Idea (*eidos*), which is equivalent to the divine Name or Attribute in Islamic theology. The spreading of these Names creates the cosmos of theophanies and manifests itself in various forms in noetic (or spiritual), psychical and physical areas.

Meanwhile, the supporters of archetypal psychology who propagate "new polytheism" (e.g. J. Hillman) perceive Hermes as a psychical archetype, whose manifestation can be explained by focusing on certain areas of human cognition and behaviour, as well as exploring the contents of dreams and unconscious fantasies. That is why A. Faivre states that Hermes is *urbis conditor*, the governor of both the material and utopian city of imagination, who governs not only the commercial domain of trade, but also the spiritual "high ground", connecting it with the world of archetypes. Hermes is a labyrinth guide and a trickster, encountered at the crossroads and transitional states of being. He is also an exile, "lost in a peripheral world of a town without East or West."[7] When talking about Hermes and his companions (Hermione, Harmonia, Iris), A. Faivre emphasizes the mobility and multifacetedness of Hermes as a guide, traveller, expert of rhetoric and hermeneut. Mercury's road is as winding as a snake entwined around a caduceus. It is not a straight line, but rather an unpredictable curve. Hermes appears not only as a treasure-revealing interpreter, but also as a secretive thief, a prankster. He is not only an escort of souls, but also a deceiver. As a patron of knowledge and science, he differentiates between real and fake philosophy, however, the knowledge

---

7. Antoine Faivre, *The Eternal Hermes. From Greek God to Alchemical Magus*, tr. by Joscelyn Godwin, Phanes Press, Grand Rapids, 1995, p. 124.

he fosters is "gnostic, eclectic, or transdisciplinary",[8] i.e. his place is somewhere between history and myth, between inspiration, fantasy and logic, as if he determines the balance of powers between Apollo and Dionysus. Mercury nearly becomes a prophet of post-modernism, secretly restoring the glory he earned at the time of the Renaissance. Such an intriguing concept of Hermes develops from psychoanalysis, alchemical Renaissance occultism and Greek mythology. It has little to do with the image of the Egyptian god Thoth.

Mercury is not only a "primary element", but also "final material"—a result of dialectic metamorphosis. He is also identified as the process of alchemical transformations itself—the curve of qualitative change. That is why the "Hermetic spirit" becomes a catalyst for psychical, cultural and social changes. C. G. Jung refers to "Mercury of the subconscious" as a "mediator" and a "saviour". However, we should not fully reject the assumption that C. G. Jung's invented "unconscious" is merely a literary fiction that marks the semiotic scope of imagination, its hypothetical horizon. Mercury the trickster sees it as the perfect dwelling place because he is depicted as a hermaphrodite (a chimeric hybrid between Hermes and Aphrodite), both a young boy (*puer*) and an old man (*senex*). Defying Aristotle's logic, he is *tertium datum*—the third path when only two are possible. Similarly to Samogitian Algis, "the messenger of gods" (*Algis angelus est summorum deorum*),[9] the mysterious Mercury reports divine decisions and revelations.

· JUPITER'S WORD AND HIS BRIDE PHILOLOGIA ·

Trying to compare Egyptian Thoth, Hellenic Hermes, and Roman Mercury caused a lot of confusion even in Antiquity.

---

8. *Ibid.*, p. 14.

9. Jonas Lasickas, *Apie žemaičių, kitų sarmatų bei netikrų krikščionių dievus*, Vaga, Vilnius, 1969, pp. 19, 40.

When trying to "historically" explain various hypostases and genealogies, many different Mercuries, who are identified as famous fictitious people, come to mind. Having in mind Antiquity's "educational rationalism" and the nature of the official Roman religion, this kind of euhemeristic hermeneutics is inevitable. In the cultural context formed by the philosophy and political rhetoric of Stoicism, academic scepticism and Epicureanism, supernatural or metaphysical beings are rarely called gods. Instead, gods are material elements and deified historical and mythological characters.

Apollonius Rhodius believed that Hermes' son Aethalides was a direct ancestor of Pythagoras (*Argonautica* I, 640f.). Plutarch of Chaeronea refers to Isis as a daughter of Hermes, while Cicero, in his work *On the Nature of the Gods*, claims that, instead of one, there were actually five Mercuries. It is the fifth hero who defeated the hundred-eyed giant Argus, fled to Egypt and was titled Thoth. He gave Egyptians the alphabet and created the laws (*De natura deorum* III.22). This peculiar legend was probably created as a narrative to justify political hegemony and the supremacy of Greek-Roman culture.

The abundant versions of Hermes were influenced not only by a myriad of Hermes-related archetypes, but also by the mythology that reflected the cultural priorities and political realities of the Roman Empire. For this reason, it is unsurprising that the image of Hermes, which emerged in the imagination of early Christians, is also two-fold. "On one hand he was condemned, ridiculed, and turned into a devil; on the other, was recognized as a benefactor, an exemplar of humane values and Christian virtues, even an image of Christ".[10]

For example, Lactantius (who, in 317 AD, was invited to educate the son of Constantine the Great), refers to Hermes as an ancient person who, as a result of his extensive education, was called Trismegistus. It is said that Hermes wrote many books about divine topics, expressing the supremacy of a single,

---

10. Antoine Faivre, *The Eternal Hermes. From Greek God to Alchemical Magus*, tr. by Joscelyn Godwin, Phanes Press, Grand Rapids, 1995, p. 22.

almighty God. The Egyptian Mercury calls this God "Father" (*Div. inst.* IV.6), which means that Hermes' teachings confirm the truths of Christianity. Lactantius states that Trismegistus (whom he regards as a prophet that foresaw the coming of Christianity) lived long before Plato or Pythagoras (*De ira Dei* XI). Lactantius compares the demiurgical Word, mentioned in Hermetic writings, with the Son of God. However, the Hermetic dialogue *Asclepius: The Perfect Discourse*, which Lactantius refers to as a prophecy of the Son of God, laments the old Egyptian religion and discusses the creation of sacred statues and images. On the contrary, Lactantius condemns the worship of images and associates the spirits, that ritualistically inhabit statues, with fallen angels (*Div. inst.* II.15). He does not want to associate Trismegistus, the master of divine truths, with these heretic sins.

The image of Mercury, created by a Carthaginian neoplatonic Martianus Capella in *The Marriage of Philology and Mercury* (fifth century AD), sparked the imagination of Medieval Christian intellectuals. In this work, the immortal Mercury represents divine eloquence, while the mortal Philology, deified by marriage and its related theurgical rituals, is the daughter of natural human mind and ingenuity (*phronesis*). She revealed to Plato and Pythagoras that celestial bodies are of spiritual essence (*De nuptiis* II.125). Mercury's handmaidens represent the seven liberal arts, while Philology's handmaidens the seven mantic arts. This is how Jupiter describes Mercury: "He is our lyre, our speech, our kindness and true genius... interpreter of our minds" (*De nuptiis* I.92).

Mercury is the word (*sermo*) of Jupiter, but his real name is Thout. Philology reveals the meaning behind Mercury's name by using gematria: when the letters of the Egyptian name *Thout* are turned into numbers, we get 1218 (i.e. 9 + 800 + 400 + 9 = 1218). With the help of some further arithmological calculations, it becomes apparent that Thout's number is 4, whereas Philology's number is 3. The sum ("marriage") of these numbers is 7—the number of divine intelligence (*Nous*), represented by Athena or Minerva (*ibid.*, II, 108).

The seven liberal arts (or sciences, *disciplinae cyclicae*), rec-
ognised by Martianus Capella and protected by Mercury—
grammar, dialectic, rhetoric, arithmetic, geometry, astronomy
and music—emerge from the Intellect, equivalent to Mercury
Trismegistus. That is why their noetic prototypes are free
from the realities of human existence, controlled by mantics
and theurgy, the means of ascension to the world of gods.
As it is stated by I. Hadot, the concept of the seven liberal
arts, so popular during the Middle Ages, was formed with the
influence of Hellenic Neoplatonists (especially Porphyry).
However, the inception of its different versions are rooted in
Middle Platonism.[11]

By referring to Mercury as language (*sermo*) and mind
(*ratio*), Christian authors emphasised the role of this god in
the area of rhetorical and allegorical interpretations. In fact,
Hermes-Word was compared to Christ-Word even in the first
centuries of Christianity. Just like Hermes guides souls into
the world of the dead, Christ leads souls into salvation. That
is why, in an attempt to preserve the supremacy of Christian
avatar, Hermes was given the title of *angelus bonus*. Byzantines
believed that he was Archangel Michael or Gabriel. Copts
even tried to depict him as a being with the head of a dog,
just like Anubis (Anpu), the Egyptian god of the dead and
embalming, or the Hellenic god Hermanubis, an iconographic fusion between Hermes and Anubis. In Dante's poetry, the
function of Hermes as the escort of souls is performed by
Virgil, the symbol of human reason, while the seven liberal
arts are presented as the seven Heavenly bodies. Here, the
planet Mercury is the patron of dialectics.

In contrast, St Augustine of Hippo, whose works had a
great influence on the adaptation of the seven liberal arts in
Christianity, partly condemns "the Egyptian Hermes, called
Trismegistus". According to St Augustine, Hermes claims that
the visible, material idols are the bodies of gods, inhabited

---

11. Ilsetraut Hadot, *Arts libéraux et philosophie dans la pensée antique*,
Études Augustiniennes, Paris, 1984, p. 137–155.

and animated by spirits (*De civ. Dei* VIII.23; cf. *Asclep.* 23–24). St Augustine dislikes this theory of liturgical rituals of Ancient Egyptian temples, preferring the triumph of the Biblical god:

> See, the Lord rides on a swift cloud
> and is coming to Egypt.
> The idols of Egypt tremble before him,
> and the hearts of the Egyptians melt with fear.
>
> "I will stir up Egyptian against Egyptian—
> brother will fight against brother,
> neighbor against neighbor,
> city against city,
> kingdom against kingdom.
>
> The Egyptians will lose heart,
> and I will bring their plans to nothing;
> they will consult the idols and the spirits of the dead,
> the mediums and the spiritists.
> (*Is.* 19. 1-3)

However, when reinterpreted literally from the perspective of Christian demonology, "Hermes tells a lot of truth about God" (*De civ. Dei* VIII.23). It is ironic that the ritualistic aspect of Hermeticism, so criticised by St Augustine, is the one that attracted humanists of the Italian Renaissance.

· MERCURY'S AND MOSES' RIVALRY IN FLORENCE ·

The so-called Renaissance, which was "discovered" or even partly "created" by nineteenth-century historians like J. Burckhardt, did not really resemble the "humanistic Arcadia", so often depicted by classicist enlighteners and rationalists. Quite the contrary—it was an age of rediscovered Hermeticism, reinterpreted Neoplatonism, astrology and talismanic magic. In other words, "Renaissance" signified a movement of individuals and closed aristocratic communities that spread their ideas about "natural magic" (*Magia Naturalis*). Both the Reformation and Counter-Reformation attempted to suppress this movement.

The Renaissance of Western occultism, as well as the onset of social power-seeking esoteric teachings (consisting of infantile utopias and peculiar pieces of mythical thinking), were partly triggered by two important events. One of them was the discovery of the Hermetic collection, brought from the Byzantine Empire after its fall in 1453. The other was the spread of Jewish Kabbalah in Europe after the Granada War. Medieval Europe knew only *Asclepius*, often mistakenly attributed to Apuleius. Around the year 1460, a monk called Leonardo (one of the manuscript collectors commissioned by Cosimo de' Medici) brought an incomplete Greek version of *Corpus Hermeticum* from Macedonia to Florence. This event attracted a lot of attention. By the command of Cosimo de' Medici, Marcilio Ficino had to postpone the translation of Plato in favour of the collection, brought from the former Byzantine Empire. The works of Trismegistus seemed much more important than Plato's *Symposium*. The translation of *Corpus Hermeticum* was completed by 1463—luckily, Ficino was able to finish the job before the death of his patron Cosimo in 1464.

Renaissance philosophers and intellectuals, who followed *Asclepius* and cherished a vision of a primordial "golden age", were lured by the promise of Egyptian wisdom. To them, the human being was "the great miracle" (*magnum miraculum*), full of hidden magical powers. And, as Mercury precedes Plato, his wisdom is considered closer to the divine source. This mythologised obsession over "Christian historicism", which values information based on its age and its closeness to the envisioned wisdom of Adam, not only raised the value of Hermetic texts, but also played a major role in their discreditation. When it emerged that the glorified "pagan" text might be written after the announcement of the "good news", its lack of mention of Christ meant that it was worthless or, even worse, a deception created by the devil himself. Also, how can one worship Hermes or Asclepius after the Son of God had revealed the absolute truth? From a fundamentalist point of view (determined by historical and theological mythologems rather than metaphysics), Hermes Trismegistus matters only in association with Moses. This idea simply reflects Judaic stories from the Ptolemaic era (for example, by Artapanus), which claim that Jewish prophets greatly influenced Hellenic philosophy. The Christians of Late Antiquity, who fiercely fought against "paganism", were in favour of all the ideological narratives like the one that said that even Plato was influenced by Moses (or that he, according to Numenius, was "an atticizing Moses").

However, the magicians and intellectuals of the Renaissance were astounded by the awe-inspiring assumption that Hermes might be older than Moses himself. Or, maybe Moses and Hermes were contemporaries? All this pseudohistorical dilemma and its resolution had great significance. That is because the interpretation of the Book of Genesis and its comparison with Hermetic cosmogony influenced the majority of cosmological speculations and the paradigm of the whole culture (as well as "authoritative" points of reference and the scope of imagination). If Hermetic cosmogony is actually older and, in turn, more authoritative (as it is closer to primordial heaven), this fact opens wide possibilities for Hermetic magic and a new perspective for "natural theology" and "perennial wisdom", which does not clash with the essence of Christianity. It is an alluring marriage of theurgy and mind, the great reconciliation of Christian and pagan wisdom (the latter wearing a worn Platonic cloak). Unfortunately, this very threat of both magic synthesis and a breakthrough of alchemical imagination forced secular and religious authorities to physically eliminate such Renaissance apostles and Egypt-admirers like Giordano Bruno, who claimed that *prisca magia* was not only a new universal philosophy, but also the true religion. The cosmogony of *Poimandres* simply did not have the right to alter, complement, or, especially, replace the cosmogony of Moses (i.e. the Old Testament's story of Genesis). That is why the Reformed church, Puritans and humanists

15

united against the Hermetic imagination, so praised by the magicians of the Renaissance.

As a self-proclaimed expert, St Augustine had a strong opinion on the rivalry between Moses and Mercury. According to him, even though Trismegistus was a predecessor of Hellenic philosophers, he lived after Abraham, Isaac, Jacob, Joseph and Moses, "for Moses was a contemporary of Atlas, Prometheus' brother, the eminent astronomer, the maternal grandfather of Mercury the elder of whom Mercury Trismegistus was the grandson" (*De civ. Dei* XVIII.29). According to St Augustine, Egyptians had no moral philosophy before Trismegistus— only astronomy.

Christians created this kind of fantastical genealogies in order to combine the stories of Hellenic and Biblical characters. Modern readers might find these attempts naively ingenious and aesthetically charming. Here are some examples written by Clement of Alexandria (2nd–3rd centuries AD):

"From Adam to the Flood comprises 2148 years four days" (*Stromateis* I.140).

"It is proven therefore that Moses lived 604 years before the reception of Dionysus among the gods, if he really was received among the gods in the thirty-second year of the reign of King Perseus, as Apollodorus reports in his *Chronica*. From Dionysus to Heracles and the heroes who sailed with Jason in the *Argo* is reckoned at sixty-three years in all. Asclepius and the Dioscuri sailed with them, as Apollonius of Rhodes records in his *Argonautica*" (*ibid.*, I.105.1-3).

"Cadmus, Semele's father, came to Thebes in the time of Lynceus and invented the Greek alphabet. Triopas was contemporary with Isis in the seventh generation after Inachus (Isis is also called "Io" through her 'going' wandering over all the earth). Istrus in his book *On the Migration of the Egyptians* says that she was daughter to Prometheus. But Prometheus was a contemporary of Triopas in the seventh generation after Moses" (*ibid.* I.160.1–2).

"From Moses' taking up command (i.e. from Inachus) to Deucalion's flood (I mean the second deluge) and the great fire caused by Phaethon which took place in the time of Crotopus adds up to eight generations; three generations make up a century. From the flood to the great fire of Ida, the discovery of metal, and the Dactyls of Ida, seventy-three years according to Thrasyllus. From the great fire of Ida to the rape of Ganymede, sixty-five years" (*ibid.* I.136.3–5).

Mythical Semitic patriarchs, heroes of Greek mythology, and Egyptian gods are all integral parts of Christian history, finally blessed with the coming of the Son of God. In this magical world, where Zeus abducts Ganymede, Io transforms into a cow and Moses surpasses Pharaoh's magicians, the coming of Christ does not seem out of place. After all, even Homer writes that gods often visit our world in the guise of ordinary people.

However, let's get back to Trismegistus. When Marsilio Ficino familiarises with the works of Proclus Diadochus, a fifth-century Neoplatonist philosopher, he customises Proclus' list of wisdom successors by including Zoroaster and Mercury. According to Proclus, "all the Greek theology is the child of Orphic mystagogy; Pythagoras was the first to receive initiation from Aglaophamos, Plato in turn received from the Pythagorean and Orphic doctrines perfect knowledge concerning the gods"[12] (*Plat. Theol.* I.5.25.26–26.4).

Ficino similarly describes Mercury, the founder of Hermopolis, a divine sage, an exceptional philosopher, the "Thrice-Great" (*termaximus*). This is his suggested chain of theological wisdom successors: Zoroaster, Mercury Trismegistus, Orpheus, Aglaophamos, Pythagoras, Plato, Philolaus. Even though Gemistos Plethon, a Byzantine philosopher, emphasises the superiority of the mythical Zoroaster, Ficino chooses Mercury as "the first theologian". He states that there

---

12. Algis Uždavinys, *Versmių labirintai. Proklo hermeneutinė filosofija ir mistagogija*, Eugrimas, Vilnius, 2002, p. 117–118.

is only one "ancient theology" (*prisca theologia*), founded by Mercury and succeeded by the divine Plato. Hence, Hermes is the founder of the perpetual tradition of wisdom, its *fons et origo*. He is not only a philosopher, an author of numerous works, but also a prophet who foresaw the coming of Christ.

According to Ficino, two of Mercury's works — *Asclepius* and *Corpus Hermeticum* — are truly divine. He assumed that these texts were originally written in the Egyptian language and later translated into Greek; that is why they reveal the sacred mysteries of Ancient Egypt. According to F. A. Yates, "Ficino believes, [that] there shines a light of divine illumination. It teaches us how, rising above the deceptions of sense and the clouds of fantasy, we are to turn our mind to the Divine Mind, as the moon turns to the sun, so that Pimander, that is the Divine Mind, may flow into our mind and we may contemplate the order of all things as they exist in God."[13] The *Corpus Hermeticum*, translated by Ficino into Latin, was first published in 1471 and republished sixteen more times by the end of the sixteenth century. In 1548, even an Italian translation by Tommaso Benci emerged in Florence.

· THE PERENNIAL PHILOSOPHY OF HERMES
AND ZOROASTER ·

With the influence of Neoplatonic and Hermetic texts, there emerged the concept of esoteric Tradition, or Perennial philosophy. More accurately, it was actually its Western Renaissance version, as ancient Greek historians and philosophers had already discussed the notion of unity between wisdom traditions—from Megasthenes, the ambassador of Seleucus I in India (c. 350 – c. 290 BC), to Numenius, Porphyry and Damascius. The term *philosophia perennis* ("perennial philosophy"), dear to modern traditionalists, was

---

13. Frances A. Yates, *Giordano Bruno and the Hermetic Tradition*, The University of Chicago Press, Chicago, 1964, p. 16.

coined by Agostino Steuco in his book *De perenni Philosophia* (1540). This "perennial philosophy", equivalent to "ancient theology" (*prisca theologia*), was associated with the name of Hermes Trismegistus. However, the supporters of Biblical history dedicated the most important place in the pantheon to the mythical Jewish patriarchs, thus "the typical roster, or 'philosophical' genealogy, took shape as follows: Enoch, Abraham, Noah, Zoroaster, Moses, Hermes Trismegistus, the Brahmins, the Druids, David, Orpheus, Pythagoras, Plato, the Sibyls."[14]

In this retrospect of "ancient theology", no one differentiated between myth and reality. The "history" of wisdom was supported by a symbolic chronology, which was nevertheless often perceived as literal: the antiquity of a character raised the value of their teachings. For this reason, if one wants to discredit the metaphysical and cosmological truths, related to a particular character, all it takes is to criticise this mythical chronology. Renaissance thinkers, for example, attributed the *Chaldean Oracles* to Zoroaster, even though the texts were created in the second and third century and represented Middle Platonism.[15] According to C. Bamford, it was the influence of Georgius Gemistos Plethon, a mystagogue who visited Florence in 1438–1439 and spread the idea of esoteric roster. The endless chain of wisdom (like the Sufi *silsilah*) is started by Zoroaster and is continued by Hermes, Orpheus, Eumolpus (the founder of the Eleusinian mysteries), Menes (the first king of Egypt), Minas (the lawgiver of Crete), Numa, the Brahmins, the mages of Media, the oracles of Dodona, Tiresias, Chiron and the Seven Sages of Greece. Pythagoras, Plato and their followers come next.

H. Corbin notes that Plethon's views are akin to the philosophy of Shahab al-Din Yahya ibn Habash Suhrawardi,

---

14. Antoine Faivre, *The Eternal Hermes. From Greek God to Alchemical Magus*, tr. by Joscelyn Godwin, Phanes Press, Grand Rapids, 1995, p. 39.

15. Christopher Bamford, "The Dream of Gemistos Plethon". *Sphinx 6*, London, 1993, p. 49.

the Master of Illumination (*shaykh al-ishrāq*), executed in Aleppo in 1191. Their suggested genealogies of "perennial wisdom" are also partly related.[16] Eliseus, the teacher who introduced Plethon to Zoroaster, was probably influenced by the ideas of al-Suhrawardi instead of the ideas of Averroes. The "Theosophy of Illumination" of al-Suhrawardi and his followers might have served as one of the prototypes for Plethon's philosophy, which emphasized both "Zoroastrian" and "Platonic" concepts.

When discussing the "science of Illumination", "symbolic wisdom" and theurgic "enlightenment" (*ta'alluh*), al-Suhrawardi mentions his predecessors who "threaded the path of God": from Hermes ("the father of philosophers") and Persian philosophers like Jamasp, to Empedocles, Pythagoras and Plato, "the leader of philosophers" (*Ḥikmat al-ishrāq* I.4).

S. H. Nasr reconstructs al-Suhrawardi's chain of wisdom from Hermes to al-Suhrawardi himself. The list begins with Hermes (prophet Idris) and Agathodaemon (prophet Set). Then, the chain (*silsilah*) splits into two branches: Egyptian and Persian. This ancient wisdom (*al-ḥikmah al-'atīqa*), also called sacred wisdom (*al-ḥikmah al-laduniyya*), travels from Egypt to Greece and is later adopted by the Islamic civilisation. After Agathodaemon, the branch of Egypt and Greece mentions Asclepius, Pythagoras, Empedocles, Plato and Neoplatonist philosophers, whose work is continued by Sufis Dhu'l-Nun al-Misri and Sahl al-Tustari. The Persian branch includes the mythical Iranian kings Keyumars (referred to as the first human being in the world), Fereydun and Kay Khosrow, as well as Islamic Sufis Abu Yazid al-Bistami, Mansur Al-Hallaj and Abu al-Hassan al-Kharaqani.[17]

---

16. Henry Corbin, *En Islam iranien. Aspects spirituels et philosophiques, tome II; Sohrawardi et les Platoniciens de Perse*, Gallimard, Paris, 1971, p. 32–36.

17. Seyyed Hossein Nasr, *Three Muslim Sages. Avicenna–Suhrawardi–Ibn 'Arabi*, Harvard University Press, Cambridge, Mass., 1964, p. 62.

Al-Suhrawardi created his distinctive Light ontology and his teachings about angelology[18] by using elements from Zoroastrianism, Egyptian Hermeticism, Platonism (*the Enneads* by Plotinus),[19] Islamic Sufism and Aristotelianism (improved by Ibn Sina). One Arabian author "connected the Ishraqiyun with a class of Egyptian priests called 'children of the sister of Hermes.'"[20]

It might be that Gemistos Plethon studied from similar sources, as the "Oriental" (*ishraq*) wisdom of al-Suhrawardi is merely a version of Persian platonism, integrated into the Islamic philosophical tradition. The name of Zoroaster, which came from syncretic Hellenism and the Sasanian culture, in this case does not indicate a historical figure, but is rather used as *auctoritas*, a password and a talisman. In the period of the Achaemenid Empire and the Seleucid Empire, a synthesis of Chaldean and Iranian teachings was formed. Thanks to it, the "iconic" name of Zoroaster found its place in philosophical and alchemical Greek literature.

From this tradition (also called "Chaldean teachings" or "Assyrian doctrines") and Middle Platonism, there appeared *the Chaldean Oracles*. Written by Julian the Chaldean, this poem is a philosophical manifestation of gods (Apollo, Hecate, and, possibly, the soul of Plato speaking from the afterlife) written in hexameter. However, only a few fragments of this poem survived in quotations by Neoplatonists like Proclus and Damascius. After more than a thousand years from the era of Julian the Chaldean and his son Julian the Theurgist, Gemistos Plethon attributed *the Chaldean Oracles* to Zoroaster. That is why Zoroaster is constantly mentioned together with Mercury in the works of Ficino—the mage

---

18. Algis Uždavinys, "Al-Suhravardžio filosofijos ypatumai". *Logos*, 2000, no. 22, p. 16.

19. Algis Uždavinys, "Divine Light in Plotinus and al-Suhrawardi", *Sacred Web. A Journal of Tradition and Modernity*, no. 10, Vancouver, Canada, 2003, p. 73.

20. Henry Corbin, *Avicenna and the Visionary Recital*, tr. W. R. Trask, Bollingen Series LXVI, Princeton University Press, 1988, p. 38.

and theologist of perennial wisdom has little to do with the
Iranian Zarathushtra, except for his Hellenised name.

· THE ASTROLOGICAL MODEL OF THE WORLD ·

In the Arabian tradition, Roger Bacon refers to Hermes
Trismegistus as the "father of philosophers". The alchemists
of the Late Middle Ages adopt the popular Islamic idea that
there were actually three Hermes: Enoch, Noah and *Hermes
Mercurius Triplex*, an Egyptian king, philosopher and prophet, who ruled Egypt after the Great Flood. The latter is unani-
mously associated with alchemy and talismanic magic. That
is why, during the Middle Ages, the books of Mercury were
not only read only in secret, but were also strictly censored or
destroyed.

However, under the influence of Hermetic and Platonic
texts brought from the Byzantine Empire, Italian thinkers of
the Renaissance changed the status of magic by contrasting
theurgical magic with black magic, as the authority of the
former was supported by "ancient theologists" (*prisci theologi,
prisci magi*)—Mercury, Zoroaster and Orpheus—while the latter was based on mere ignorance. If Neoplatonist philosopher
Iamblichus had been resurrected at that moment, he would
have been upset that the men of the Renaissance referred to
this modified theurgy with the incorrect term of *magia naturalis*, thus causing confusion, as the terms of Platonic and
Chaldean *theourgia* (ritualistic "working of the gods") were
clearly differentiated in Late Antiquity.

Renaissance occultism operated under the name of
Egyptian theology. By proclaiming Copernicus' Sun as the
visible Neoplatonist image of the One, Giordano Bruno propagated his astrological talismanic magic as natural Egyptian
religion and indisputable wisdom. Since Christianity and
Judaism were irreparably corrupted, one must return to their
Egyptian origins and reform the world with the help of noetic
Sun's magic, the sorcery of stars-archetypes, hieroglyphs, geometric shapes, colours and numbers. Here, Hermes-Mercury

is the central figure—the prophet of the Sun of the sacred intellect, which shines beyond the visible Sun.

When talking about the kindred of the cosmogonies of Moses and Egyptian Mercury, Ficino is certain that the cosmogony of Poimandres is the superior one. Trismegistus surpasses Moses because he equates the demiurgical Word with the Son of God, as if he foresees the incarnation of Christ. Sometimes, Ficino asks himself: if Mercury revealed the whole truth about the creation of the world, maybe he is Moses, just like the Jewish historian Artapanus claimed? (*Theologia Platonica* VIII.1) However, this hypothesis should be dismissed because Moses' teachings and the Egyptian doctrine about the creation of the cosmos differ in terms of the treatment of the human being. Egyptian Adam is not a slave made from earthly dust. Instead, he is a divine being belonging to the world of stars; he is the brother of the Son of God, or the demiurgical Word. His downfall is merely a descent into the material realm governed by planets, as well as a division into two opposite genders, as is written in Plato's *Symposium*. However, the immortal half of this daemonic Human remains unchanged, just like the higher part of the soul in Plotinus' philosophy.

According to Ficino, the human being can defy the power of "the Seven Governors" that rule the physical domain, because the human intellect (*mens*), which reflects the wholeness of divine Intellect, is not subject to nature. Nature itself is a mere reflection of higher realities; that is why understanding the sympathetic and analogue structure of this image allows us to change the composition of the elements of both the physical and psychical worlds—to improve or to worsen their state. The aim of philosophical Hermeticism is to surpass the material (psychosomatic) domain, while the aim of alchemical and magical Hermeticism (if we find this kind of division of terms acceptable) is to "scientifically" rearrange this destiny-controlled domain and to use it for positive purposes.

Renaissance image magic requires a certain model of the world in which the cosmic absoluteness, arising from the One, is imagined as an orb divided into strata and sections. The geometric construction of this absoluteness is identical to the astronomical construction of the material universe. By the example of Ptolemy, Plato and Aristotle, the latter is depicted as a hierarchy of seven planets, crowned with a sphere full of attached stars. Beyond it, there lie metaphysical prototypes and divine archetypes. The Earth exists in the centre of this imaginary orb, which is permeated by a multifaceted stream of divine influences. This stream itself is "filtered" and partly transformed by the screen of each planetary sphere, ruled by its respective god and his servants. The world of archetypes (or Platonic Ideas) is arranged as a circle, articulated by the system of astrological signs.

All this spatial composition looks like an architectural construction, both static and dynamic at the same time. The structure of the visible cosmos imitates the structure of the invisible cosmos of prototypes. Only this kind of theophanic Universe allows for the discussion of "working of the stars", because stars here exist as soul archetypes and visible forms of gods. Thanks to its definite form (including the rings of the seven planets that surround the sublunary area), this universe represents a Hellenistic, not ancient Egyptian cosmography. However, the Egyptians perceived their country as an image of Heaven and a temple of the eternal gods (*neteru*).

If we, by the Egyptian example, divide the circle of Heaven into 360 sections (which are ruled by 36 gods, or decans), we get a sufficient model of the cosmological Year, as imitated by the sacred calendar. Additionally, the 36 decans (*bakiu*) are directly related to the 36 districts of Egypt, i.e. the "body" parts of the country-temple. The whole day of this conscious ritualistic organism is governed and protected by different deities of varying ranks. A day is divided into 12 hours of daytime and 12 hours of night time. Each hour is governed by different constellations of gods. That is why the diurnal cycle can be regarded as a rite of the transcendental and immanent pantheon of existence. The mythical precedents of these rites compose the iconostasis of the sun god Ra's (demiurgical Intelligence) navigational stops, or episodes. The material cosmical organism is the reflection (*tut*) of sacred nonmaterial lights. It functions as a community of spiritual, psychical and physical essences, as a system of substantial "names", governed by the perennial truth (*maat*) and ontological "magic" (*heka*). All its parts work in accordance to each other. Renaissance mages studied similar cosmologies from the works of the Late Antiquity that had been reinterpreted and edited numerous times. At that time, all the science of Islam and Christianity was based on those reedited works.

The cosmic circle rotates in an orderly manner, and that is why it is possible to "scientifically" predict the change of the composition of being. The Egyptian cosmographical model of 36 decans and 24 hours was supplemented with by the system of the twelve Zodiac signs, which came from Mesopotamia though the Greeks and the Persians. From a metaphysical point of view, planets and stars (similarly to temple statues) are merely the visible forms of invisible gods; that is why the physical world is actually affected by divine archetypes, which exist both "everywhere and nowhere". Cosmology plays the role of a supplementary symbolic model. It is like a diagram that classifies the attributes of cosmic absoluteness, spiritual virtues and the quality of material objects.

However, there is always the esoteric temptation to perceive this symbolic mandala in the literal sense by thinking that a planet (which is the mask of the epiphanies of a specific god) functions as a physical body. As long as this spiritual "schema" (naively compared to the visible astronomical cosmos) is not ruined by new cosmology, it functions as an "objective" projection of the imagination, covering the whole material reality. Mythological consciousness perceives Celestial bodies as live supernatural entities; that is why, for example, the reins of destiny are held by the hostile archons in gnostic cosmology. How do contemporary astrologers manage to transfer this, both mythical and cosmological-calendrical, model (based on divine hierarchy or demonology) into astronomical post-Descartes space and explain it as the action of "inanimate material bodies"? This is a mystery that can be solved only by an experienced political demagogue, who knows that human stupidity and gullibility are infinite.

In this way, vague suspicions and the desire to experience a tangible effect of providence (or to trick the primitively-imagined mechanism of fate) are expressed in the language of aesthetic-psychological syncretism, which attempts to lean towards materialist cosmology.

According to the Hermeticists of the Renaissance, the decans who use daemons and planets as visible masks are actually divine powerful forces, located above the Zodiac circle that surrounds the visible cosmos. The rays that radiate from the circle of Absoluteness form separate dispersive chains, thus connecting the essences, beings, objects and images with their respective decan, or monad. Sympathetic and analogous bonds can connect all things with their demiurgic archetypes and, in turn, influence them. During the Renaissance, Hermes Trismegistus was believed to be the author of various treatises about astrological medicine, the names and powers of the Zodiac signs, and the occult characteristics of animals. It was believed that, with the help of talismans and symbols, one can control their fate by influencing the powers that channel in archetypal trajectories—to fall ill or to recover, to obtain desired qualities and spiritual attributes, to experience favours or disfavours. By knowing the "perennial" names and symbols of decans, it is possible to determine the theurgic connection between the levels of reality governed by these decans. That is why Hermes' *Sacred Book* (*Liber sacer*) not only depicts the magical images of decans and the list of their respective stones and plants, but also teaches how to correctly carve their symbols on carefully selected materials, how to craft rings and what rules one should follow while wearing them.

· THE MIRACULOUS CITY OF HERMES TRISMEGISTUS ·

Numerous Renaissance artists and thinkers were influenced by a certain book, attributed to Hermes Trismegistus. In Europe, this book was known by the curious name of *Picatrix*.

The metaphysical basis of this work is Neoplatonic philosophy mixed with peripatetic and stoic physics.

Where did this work come from? Actually, it is a shortened translation of an Arabic text, *The Goal of the Wise (Ghāyat al-ḥakīm)*, about the Hermetic magic of the Sabians. A part of it consists of excerpts from *The Book of Nabataean Agriculture (Kitāb al-Filāḥa al-nabatiyya)*, which contains a lot of information on the occult. The Arabic text claims that this treatise is translated from the Chaldean language, however, it seems that the original was written in Greek and was partly based on the esoteric traditions of the Middle East. It is thought that this work was most likely compiled from several sources by Abu Talib Ahmad ibn al-Zayyat.

Picatrix begins with some prayers and the promise to reveal the mysteries of reality. There appears the motive of "knowledge", so well-liked by the Gnostics—however, the hierarchy of existence depicted in *Picatrix* imitates the structure of Neoplatonic hypostases. Here, the highest truth is nonmaterial and identical to the One, which is the origin of the existence and which represents divine unity. Meanwhile, the structure of existence is controlled by the axes of descendance and ascendance: the elements of the higher plane descend into the lower plane and illuminate it, while the elements of the latter ascend. While existing as "the minor world", the human being actually reflects "the major world" and its structure. However, in terms of intellect, he transcends the seven heavenly spheres, i.e. the domain governed by planets. The knowledge of the origin of everything, granted by God, is the basis of the magical art of reflections.

The mentioned work states that three types of emanations arise from the formless One: 1) *Intellectus*, 2) *Spiritus*, 3) *Materia*. Just like the divine *bau* descend into their material bodies and images in Egyptian cosmology, *spiritus* descend into material recipients, giving them a shape and granting power. The form and attributes of an earthly material object directly depend on the form of its respective celestial substance. The connection between these two cosmic planes is supported by the effect of "spiritual" (*spiritus*) rays. That is

27

why the art of magic is actually the ability to catch the effects of *spiritus* and channel them in a desired direction by adjusting the ray trajectories.

The structural entirety of the cosmos of manifestations is regarded as an integral hierarchy of forms and reflections, as a perfect geometrical structure, permeated by the holy spirit from beginning to end. For this reason, all the features, shapes, positions, and time segments of specific objects have their corresponding prototypes and higher-plane duplicates. Therefore, symbolic depictions of objects, carved at the right time into the right material, function as antennas and transmitters that allow to receive and alter the effects of archetypes. Metaphysics, mythology, mathematics, astronomy, music and planetary daemonology function as a theoretical framework for cosmological magic and talisman crafting. By taking this framework into account, a "philosopher" can scientifically draw their imaginative universe together with the emblems that compose it.

The first two books of *Picatrix* discuss the talismans depicting the planets and the thirty six decans. The third book determines the relationship of various objects and concepts (including body parts, names, colours, as well as the qualities of plants, animals and minerals) with specific celestial bodies and their iconographic symbols. The fourth one talks about purification with the help of incense.

In the fourth book of *Picatrix*, Hermes Trismegistus is introduced as the patron of image magic and the founder of a wonderful city. In the Latin version, this city is called Adocentyn, while the Arabic version calls it al-Ashmunayn, which is, most likely, another name for Hermopolis, the centre of worship for Thoth. Its image is related to the prophecy of Asclepius that mentions the construction of an ideal city in the West of Egypt. One might think that this utopian city is in Amentet, or the Duat—the Underworld, which is regarded as the domain of the magic of cosmic Imagination (*heka*), situated between the light of spiritual archetypes and the world of material bodies—or the temple of Osiris, modelled after the prototype of the solar Intellect.

In *Picatrix*, Egyptian Hermes is directly linked to the art of symbolic images and theurgical talismans:

> The Chaldeans, indeed, were those magi who made themselves preeminent in this science and these workings; and they are held to have been entirely perfect in this science. They themselves assert that Hermes first constructed a certain house of images, from which he used to measure the flow of the Nile at the Mountains of the Moon; but this house was made of the Sun. He used to hide himself there from men in such a way that no one who was with him was able to see him. He also built, in the east of Egypt, a city twelve miles in length, in which he built a certain citadel that had four gates in its four quarters. At the eastern gate he put the image of an eagle, at the western gate the image of a bull, at the southern gate the image of a lion, and at the northern gate he built the image of a dog. He made certain spiritual essences enter into these, which used to speak in voices that issued from the images; nor could anyone pass through the portals without their permission. In that city he planted certain trees, in the midst of which he set up an arbor that bore the fruits of all generations. At the summit of the citadel he caused to be built a certain tower, which attained a height of thirty cubits, and on the summit of it he commanded to be put a sphere, the color of which changed in every one of the seven days. At the end of the seven days it received the color it had at first. Every day, that city was filled with the color of that sphere, and thus the aforesaid city used to shine every day with color. Around that tower, in a circle, water abounded, in which many kinds of fish used to live. Around the city he placed diverse and changing images, by means of which the inhabitants of the city were made virtuous and freed from sin, wickedness and sloth. The name of this city was Adocentyn. (*Picatrix* IV.3)

The idea of the temple and the cosmic city, built by Hermes Trismegistus, sparked the imagination of both Arabs and Renaissance Italians. The images that guard Adocentyn might be related either to the iconography of the thirty-six decans or the Zodiac signs that give control over the effects of the stars. Hermes' city is regarded as both the earthly micro-cosm that reflects the heavenly proto-image and as a gigantic theurgical machine that helps to harmoniously distribute the rays of the archetypes of the noetic world. Hermes' astro-logical tower catches the attention of certain Persian Muslim poets, for example, Nizami (1141–1209), who wrote a poem about Bahram Gur and the seven beauties (*Haft paikar*). In this story, Bahram's path from the black palace to the white palace symbolizes the ascent of the soul.

The image of Adocentyn is undoubtedly related to the cosmological doctrines and theurgical rituals of the Harranian Sabians. The tradition of Harranian Sabians, doc-umented by al-Biruni and al-Masudi, can be referred to as Hermeticism, which is partly based on Neopythagoreanism and Neoplatonism. This is how al-Masudi (in his historical book *The Meadows of Gold*) describes the Harranian temples that existed in the early Islamic period:

> The Harranian Sabians have temples according to the names of the intellectual substances and the stars. To these temples belong: the temples of the first cause and of Intelligence, but I do not know whether it is the first or second Intelligence; also, the temple of world order, Necessity. The temple of the soul is round; of Saturn, hexagonal; of Jupiter, triangular; of Mars, long (rectangular); the Sun square; that of Venus, a triangle in a quadrangle; that of Mercury, a triangle inside an elongated quadrangle, and that of the moon, octagonal. The Sabians have in them symbols and mysteries which they keep hidden.[21]

Al-Masudi's knowledge about Sabian rituals comes from a poem by Ibn Ayshun that mentions "the Sabian temple

---

21. *Murūj al-Dhahab* (*Les prairies d'Or*), ed. and tr. C. Barbier de Maynard, A. Pavet de Courteille, Paris 1861-1877, rpt.1962, 9 vols. Quoted from Tamara M. Green, *The City of the Moon God*, Brill, Leiden, 1992, p. 116.

which stood at the Raqqah gate and contained four under-
ground chambers in which were placed idols that represented
the different heavenly bodies and the higher beings and the
mysteries of the idols. [...] Into these chambers, the Sabians
would bring their young children who became terrified by
the strange sounds and voices which [according to al-Masudi]
seemed to come from the statues on account of the mechanical devices used to create such an effect. The guardians of
the temple, hidden behind the wall, were the source of these
utterances; and their voices, transmitted by mechanical appa-
ratus, seemed to come out of these same idols."[22]

This educative approach to the origin of "pagan super-
stitions" is based on the iconoclastic attitude of monotheism (which *a priori* denies the possibility of such a theurgical occurrence), as well as vague memories of antique plays
with moving god statues and decoration-lifting equipment.
According to Heron of Alexandria, aside from the obvious
practical benefits to civilization, science should also amaze
and intimidate. Whether the talking statues of Egyptian
temples are part of a deceptive spectacle conducted by
priests (like it was thought by Greek rationalists and bi-
ased early Christians, who gladly accepted other kinds of
miracles) is a separate question, to which there is no definite answer.

· THE MAGIC OF MARSILIO FICINO ·

Marsilio Ficino referred to Hermes Trismegistus as the predecessor of Moses. He thought that Pythagoras gained some
of Hermes' wisdom in Egypt and conveyed it to Plato, whose
Timaeus is a result of modified Hermetic teachings. That
is why, even though Ficino's concept of "natural magic" is
based on the authority of Zoroaster and Trismegistus, its
theoretical framework is composed of both Neoplatonic and

---

22. *Idem.*

31

Gnostic division of intelligence, soul and body in the levels of macrocosm and microcosm. Hence, between the demiurgic Intelligence of the World and the Body of the World, there appears the Soul of the World. The Divine Intelligence (*mens*) is beaming with Ideas, which, in the level of the Soul of the World, turn into "seminal" prototypes that Plotinus calls *logoi*. These three levels of a single "organism" are closely connected because images are directly affected and sustained by prototypes, or reasons. All of this is a combination of the doctrines of Stoicism and Middle Platonism that the Chaldeans applied to theurgical astrology.

If a material form deviates from the divine trajectory and degrades, it can be "fixed" not only on the level of the body, but also the soul. If a prototype of a higher level (its symbolic image) is manipulated, its corresponding object will also be altered. As the transitional level of the soul is a realm of imaginative concepts, it means that, with the help of a symbolic-iconographic image, it is possible to alter a material object that belongs to the vertical axis of being. The *logoi* of the Soul of the World magically governs and modifies the objects of a lower level.

It seems that Ficino often simply quotes Plotinus, especially *Enn.* IV.3.9, where statues and temples are regarded as the receivers of Soul dispersions. According to Ficino, by using the images of stars that belong to the chain of magical synergy, it is possible to affect physical forms because they are mere reflections of Soul forms. The physical forms, on their own, reflect the forms of Intelligence, or Ideas. That is why, with the right ritualistic manipulations of the iconographic images that represent the transitional domain of the Soul, one can crystalize and accumulate the dispersions of the ever-present Soul into sacred receivers—temples, god statues and icons. It is also possible to alter the configurations of lower-level bodies by adjusting the configurations of higher-level images, to magically "reform" the world.

Renaissance mages utilize ontological talismans as catchers of divine influence, using them to alter and redistribute the invisible rays of the Soul. In this way, the connections of the lower world are shifted and cosmic integrity is restored In other words, the objects of the physical world are "healed" or restored with the help of the spirit (*spiritus*). Ficino's theory of natural magic is exclusively based on this same spirit (*spiritus*). According to him, between the Soul of the World and the Body of the World there exists yet another domain, the *spiritus mundi*, through which the effects of archetypal stars reach the human being. The human spirit, which resides in the body, and the whole *corpus mundi* "absorb" these invisible substances. The connections between a human spirit and its corresponding planet's spirit are determined at the level of *spiritus*. Every mineral, animal, plant, smell, colour, even a type of food has its own *spiritus* and belongs to a complicated system of pneumatic interactions. This shares similarities with Stoicism. That is why the mage, who manipulates the elements of the domain of *spiritus*, plays the sacred role of the reformer of the world.

However, we should not forget that Ficino's *spiritus* functions between the Body and the Soul, while the divine Intelligence surpasses the Soul of the World. It is always important to keep this hierarchy in mind. When discussing Plotinus' *Enneads* and Trismegistus' *Asclepius*, Ficino writes that a material object, prepared for the effects of the higher spheres, is permeated with the ever-present force of vitality. Just like a mirror reflects the face, or an echo reflects the voice, an object, affected by the vitality of the Soul, becomes a means of magic communication. According to Ficino, Plotinus follows the example of Mercury when discussing how divine powers descend into statues:

Mercurius himself, whom Plotinus follows, says that he composed through aerial demons, not through celestial or higher demons, statues from herbs, trees, stones, aromatics having within them a natural divine power (as he says). There were skillful Egyptian priests who, when they could not persuade men by reason that there are gods, that is some spirit above men, invented that illicit magic which by enticing demons into statues made these appear to be gods... I at first thought,

33

following the opinion of the Blessed Thomas Aquinas, that if they made statues which could speak, this could not have been only through stellar influence but through demons (*De vita coelitus comparanda* 26).[23]

However, once Ficino becomes conversant with Plotinus' philosophy, he changes his opinion. Some Egyptian priests may have practiced demonic magic, but Trismegistus does not belong to this category—his hieratic magic is based on the effect of the Ideas of the demiurgical Intelligence with the mediation of celestial images, whose power is maintained by the hierarchical universal structure, governed by the Intelligence. This structure requires a mage who mediates between the higher and lower levels of reality. In this way, Plotinus' metaphysics becomes a theoretical counterpoint to the Hermetic magic of the Renaissance.

Inspired by the city of Trismegistus described in *Picatrix*, Ficino speaks about "a universal image, the image of the world" (*mundi figura*), "constructed of brass, gold and silver, those being the metals of Jupiter, the Sun and Venus". This construction is a model of the universal spheres. Similarly, Plotinus encourages the imagining of and meditating on the noetic world as a harmonious sphere, both identical to and different from itself. This kind of visualisation is a component of Plotinus' spiritual practice and has little to do with the astrological magic of the Renaissance (*Enn.* V.8.9.1-3).[24]

In the eyes of Ficino, the material *mundi figura* becomes not only a means for meditation, but also a magical redistributor of the forces of the universe. In art, *mundi figura* is symbolically replaced by the three graces, representing the Sun, Venus and Jupiter, or simply a combination of the colours blue, gold

---

23. Frances A. Yates, *Giordano Bruno and the Hermetic Tradition*, The University of Chicago Press, Chicago, 1964, p. 67.

24. Sara Rappe, "Self-Knowledge and Subjectivity in the Enneads" in *The Cambridge Companion to Plotinus*, ed.by Lloyd P. Gerson, Cambridge University Press, 1996, p. 260–261.

and green. Even the primary function of *Primavera*, a painting by Botticelli, is to represent practical magic. Symbolic iconography, figure arrangement, and the choice of colours create a talisman that radiates heavenly grace, and Botticelli's work can be perceived as such a talisman.

Ficino states that the cross can also be regarded as a magical artefact:

> The force of the heavens is greatest when the celestial rays come down perpendicularly and at right angles, that is to say, in the form of a cross joining the four cardinal points. The Egyptians hence used the form of the cross, which to them also signified the future life, and they sculptured that figure on the breast of Serapis. Ficino, however, thinks that the use of the cross among the Egyptians was not so much on account of its power in attracting the gifts of the stars, but as a prophecy of the coming of Christ, made by them unknowingly.[25]

· EMBLEMS, IMAGES AND HIEROGLYPHS ·

C. Mezzasalma equates the concept of imagination to Prometheus. He states that Ficino, by deepening his knowledge of images, imagination and fantasy, stroke a balance between Hermetism-inspired magic and Platonism—the philosophy of Plotinus, Iamblichus and Proclus.[26] Believing that even a well-performed piece of music (or a hymn of Orpheus) or an image, correctly carved on a well-chosen stone, can repair a person's bodily and spiritual health, he writes:

---

25. Frances A. Yates, *Giordano Bruno and the Hermetic Tradition*, The University of Chicago Press, Chicago, 1964, p. 73.

26. Carmelo Mezzasalma, "Marsilio Ficino's De Amore, Beauty and Eros. Beauty and Eros as Care of the Soul." *Sphinx 6*, 1993, p. 42–43.

"A lyre resonates when the strings of another lyre are played. Just like that, the similarity between a celestial body and an image, carved on an amulet, allows the image to absorb the rays from its corresponding star."[27]

In the Renaissance, an emblem-like image was regarded as a body of an idea, which helped to transform consciousness and to create psychosomatic balance. Sacred hymns, liturgy, paintings and architectural structures perform a similar function.

After finally overcoming Plato's mistrust of images, Neoplatonism (whom Renaissance thinkers merged with the remains of Hermetic and Gnostic traditions) regarded the icon (*eikōn*) as a means of approaching to noetic prototypes and divine unity. However, Greek Neoplatonists were used to approaching imagination (*phantasia*) cautiously. Instead of calling it an active creative force (like the Romanticists, who adopted Renaissance ideas), they referred to it as an intersection point of descending and ascending cosmological curves, or a double mirror that reflects both sensory impressions and the ideas of the noetic world.

Meanwhile, the Renaissance philosophy of magic gave to the image a special astrological, aesthetical and political-pedagogical value. Influenced by Neoplatonic ideas, Cristoforo Giarda (an Italian professor of rhetorics), in his work *Bibliothecae Alexandrinae Icones Symbolicae* (1626 and 1628), states that the mind, exiled from Heaven into the dark cave of the body and restrained by senses, can contemplate the beauty of the forms of Virtues and Science (conveyed through colours and liberated from the clutches of matter) with the help of emblems.[28]

The word *emblema* (pl. *emblemata*) is derived from the Greek verb *emballō*—cast into, incrust. That is what one calls

---

27. Christina Linsenmeyer-van Schalkwyk, "Musical Emblems in the Renaissance: A Survey." *Alexandria 5*, Phanes Press, 2000, p. 183.
28. *Ibid.*, p. 182.

a symbolic figure or a composition with an allegorical meaning. The term itself was coined in 1522 by Andreas Alciati, the
author of the first book on emblems. Just like a Christian icon,
an emblem consists of a combination of text and an image.
This word spread in the sixteenth century and was at times
substituted with other words like *impresa, symbolum, theatrum,
pegma*. According to C. Linsenmeyer-van Schalkwyk, an emblem is comprised of three elements: a picture of an object or
scene, a rhymed epigram, taken from a separate source and a
motto that explains the intended idea or the relation between
the picture and the epigram. With the help of this motto, a
hermeneut can reveal the symbolic meaning of the emblem.[29]

The link between a picture and literary text or, in other
words, the connection between an image and an epigram,
determines the symbolic effectiveness of an emblem. A Post-
Renaissance emblem is an emancipated and aesthetized suc-
cessor of the Hermetic talisman. It still possesses moral and
mystical intentions. Hence, it is not surprising that the relationship between a picture and an epigraph resembles that of
the body and soul. Also, interpreting an emblem allows for
polysemy, or the possibility for many different meanings and
explanations.

From the historical point of view, the art of emblems originated from gnostic gems, the magic of Hermetic talismans
and the study of the treatise *Hieroglyphica* (1505), published in
Venice and presumably written by Horapollo, one of the last
priests of Ancient Egypt. Renaissance mages believed that
the text might have been written by Horus himself. However,
it might be that the edition, signed by Horapollo and featur-
ing Western-style images, was merely an edited summary of
the original.

The Renaissance theory of the hieroglyphic script, which
discusses the spiritual influence of image and text, originates
from this specific work by Horapollo. It was later criticized
and mocked by the followers of historical positivism, who mis-

---

29. *Ibid.*, p. 176.

understood its imaginative nature and meaning. This tradition, by the example of Plotinus, perceives a hieroglyph as an archetypal figure that contains a hidden meaning and reveals the intrinsic nature of an object. Hermes-Thoth is thought to be the creator of hieroglyphs, and his magical-iconographic writing is regarded as a tool for hermetic contemplation and theurgical hermeneutics. One "reads" his writing with the help of an "imaginative semiotics" which transcends the usual linguistic procedures. According to Hermeticists, every image contains an archetype that affects the soul directly, bypassing the discursive mind without the need of logical arguments.

Athanasius Kircher (Nicolas Poussin's teacher of perspective) also regarded the ancient Egyptian religion as the source of the religion of ancient Greece and Rome, as well as the source of Jewish, Chaldean, Indian and Chinese religions. He saw both an exoteric and esoteric side in every tradition and believed that ancient Hermeticists (the followers of Trismegistus) conveyed the wisdom of Egypt to Zoroaster, Orpheus, Pythagoras, the Chaldeans and Jewish Kabbalists. Plato and Proclus advocate this same esoteric tradition. In his works *Oedipus Aegyptiacus* (1652), *Obeliscus Aegyptiacus* (1666) and *Sphinx Mystagoga* (1676), A. Kircher analyzes hieroglyphs symbolically instead of linguistically. Egyptian hieroglyphs that depict a globe, a serpent and a pair of wings are interpreted as the Egyptian triad of Emepht, Phtha and Amun, which corresponds to the Christian Trinity of Father, Son and the Holy Spirit, as well as Plotinus' triad of One-Intellect-Soul, the Orphic triad of Night-Heaven-Aether, and many others.[30]

It does not really matter if the scribes of ancient Egypt would have agreed with A. Kircher and the Hermeneuticists of Alexandria, especially given the many different possible interpretations of the same subject. In this case, hieroglyphical

---

30. Joscelyn Godwin, *Athanasius Kircher. A Renaissance Man and the Quest for Lost Knowledge*, Thames and Hudson, London, 1979, p. 19.

figures are merely a starting point for the creative imagination and the intellect. It is possible to "decipher" metaphysics even from seashells or lotus flowers. Unimaginative researchers, who project their own modernist prejudice into the past, often do not even comprehend either the archaic concepts of life and the divinity of being, or their subsequent philosophical modifications. Even if a Renaissance mage was unaware of the actual linguistic meaning behind hieroglyphs, he could still have "read" them as a "text" of initiation that transformed the unconscious and awakened the power of imagination. In this way, imagination becomes the source of revelation. It maintains a dialogue with the visualized spirit guide Hermes, or a mythical personification that represents the inner self. It is not a technology of scientific philology and grammar anymore, but one of ritual meditation.

According to one disciple of Paracelsus, magical actions can be performed with the help of the imagination, and "all the wonderful things" can be done through inherent faith, which assists in befriending the spirits. Imagination in a person functions like the Sun (the visible symbol of divine Intelligence) because, just as the physical Sun turns objects into ashes, the nonphysical consciousness of a person affects the spirit. Whatever the visible body does, the invisible body follows suit.[31]

The image of an active alchemical imagination is not a metaphor, but a "living" mythical personification of the contents that are not directly understood by the conscious mind. As stated by K. Helminski, such imagination does not produce falsehood, but rather reveals the hidden reality, thus restoring spiritual meaning to the objects of the physical realm.[32] By following the philosophical tradition of Stoics, Hermeticists and Neoplatonists (which was later modified by Sufis), the

---

31. Oswald Croll and Jeffrey Raft, "Jung and the Alchemical Imagination." *Alexandria 5*, Phanes Press, 2000, p. 221–222.
32. Kabir Helminski, "Soul Loss and Soul Making." *Alexandria 5*, Phanes Press, 2000, p. 316.

above-mentioned author emphasizes two levels of consciousness that are regarded as two separate worlds: the sensory world and the world of meanings, which surpasses the former. This means that the active imagination, which manifests itself in higher planes, can reveal the deepest meanings of both external phenomena and dreams. "The outer dream that surrounds us may be the manifestation of our own psychic fragmentation. It may be less an embodied vision than a broadcast, commercially sanctioned schizophrenia."[33]

The theory of the contemplation and interpretation of hieroglyphs, which originated from Alexandrian Hermeticism and Neoplatonism, is similar to the theory of tantric art. According to it, an image functions on both the ordinary plane and a level that transcends the empirical sense of self, or consciousness. This level can be perceived as either a daimonic or angelic world of Spiritual waves. It retransmits the primordial principles that create and sustain the physical universe. That is why the reality of *mundus imaginalis* (observable by the eye of imagination) blends into the physical reality and magically transforms its picture. This means that all arts are "political", because properly made images sustain not only the individual, but also the state with its social institutions—the whole visible universe, even. Archaic civilizations function in a similar manner—calendrical rituals and music that imitates cosmic liturgy determine the harmony and well-being of the whole "body" of a nation.

From a historical and philological point of view, the hieroglyphic theory of the Renaissance is just a mere misunderstanding. That is because it does not translate or read foreign texts but rather creates (by succumbing to aesthetic impressions) a hallucination-like semantic superstructure, which becomes a starting point for alchemical imagination. P. L. Wilson states that a logothete (in the primary sense—an administrative title in the middle and late Byzantine Empire)

---

33. *Ibid.*, p. 322.

uses words to construct a universe, in which he then starts living.

Only from the perspective of sterile modernism can we regard the Hermetic project as a failure or a nonsense that has nothing in common with seemingly "objective" methods of nominalist philology, history or archeology. Hermetic talismans that were turned into paintings and emblems continue playing the role of initiation. Books like *Hypnerotomachia Poliphili* (1499), in which images and texts create an integral symbolic-allegorical structure, are meant for meditation and "internal endeavors". They become a substitute for laboratory alchemic work. With the help of the innate "love of looking" (*scopophilia*), imagination leads the process of internal transformation and guides the soul through the labyrinths of mythological landscape and architecture. It presents allegorical figures, emblems and sights of ruins. P. L. Wilson even sees a connection between the hieroglyphic theory and the contemporary magic of advertising:

> The revolutionists of the occult—"left wing" Hermeticists—failed to implement their utopian politics by the means of projective semiotics or the hieroglyphic theory; however, advertisers had no such trouble. Nowadays, the tyranny of images has been universalized. The cosmos of pan-capitalism was sealed like some kind of a Ptolemaic universe, and that is why today all human relations are perceived in the context of economic exchange.[34]

· THE MAGICAL WORLD OF IMAGINATION ·

When talking about the active imagination, much emphasized by the Hermeticists of the Renaissance, we should not forget that, during classical Antiquity, *phantasia* usually meant the

---

34. Peter Lamborn Wilson, "Oneiriconographia: Entering Poliphilo's Utopian Dreamscape", *Alexandria 5*, Phanes Press, 2000, p. 418.

ability to passively reflect external phenomena rather than the creative power that manipulated various constructs on its own. However, Middle Platonists, who transformed the classical theory of Ideas, and their follower Origen, an exegete of Hebrew-Christian scriptures, searched for noetic, or spiritual, equivalents of the five senses.

By trying to explain why the deities of the Bible are given anthropomorphic attributes and why Christian afterlife is perceived through the lens of carnality, Origen states that the domain of divine Intellect contains counterparts to all the physical senses. This theory is based on both Middle Platonists' speculations about archetypes and the concept of "spiritual human" developed by Gnostics and Philo of Alexandria. The latter concept is a polar opposite to the extrinsic, physical human, and is perceived as an intrinsic human made in God's image (*kat' eikona—Leg. alleg.* I.31). Hence, the spiritual human body is analogous to its physical counterpart in all aspects.

Some Middle Platonists and Neoplatonists shared similar ideas. Plotinus proposed that "here" (in the world of physical bodies) the senses are merely faded and obscured intellections (*noeseis*), but "there" (in the world of intellect and prototypes) intellections are vivid sensations. According to J. Dillon, both Origen and Plotinus rely on a shared Platonic tradition that comes from Plato's interpretation of the *Faidros* myth.[35] However, we cannot dismiss the assumption that the mentioned theory, directly or indirectly, comes from Egyptian mythology, as the *Faidros* myth depicts the divine journey of gods and spirits, which imitates the ritualistic actions of Ra, the deity of the sun.

A conversation between Apollonius of Tyana (a sage of Neo-Pythagoreanism) and Tespesion the Egyptian, chronicled (or created) by a sophist Philostratus, marks a turning

---

35. John Dillon, *Aisthesis Noete: A Doctrine of Spiritual Senses in Origen and Plotinus. The Golden Chain. Studies in the Development of Platonism and Christianity*, Variorum, 1990, XXIII, p. 455.

point in the process of reestablishing the status of imagination. This episode is based on a faulty perception of the theory of Egyptian images and symbols. Nevertheless, it marks a change in the status of imagination in Hellenistic philosophy. Here, Apollonius belittles the depictions of animal-headed Egyptian gods. However, when Tespesion mockingly asks him, whether Hellenic sculptors Pheidias and Praxiteles have been to Heaven to witness the real appearance of the gods, Apollonius retaliates that Hellenic sculptures are designed with the help of imagination (*phantasia*), not imitation (*mimesis*). That is because imagination can see the invisible.

Today, such a comparison seems like a misunderstanding. After all, the portrayal of Anubis, compared to the anthropomorphic depictions of Zeus or Apollo, makes it obvious that Egyptian iconography and style are exclusively based on symbolic imagination. It seems that Apollonius does not understand this at all—he is just a means for Roman intellectuals who want to convey a new definition of imagination.

Neoplatonist philosopher Proclus, in turn, writes about verbally expressed imagination (*lektike phantasia*), which creates names that construct the fabric of reality itself. The creator of these names is the divine Intellect (*nous*), and that is why they are equivalent to paradigms (*eikones*—*In Crat.* 19.22-23). At the microcosmic level, names are the products of "an imaginative soul" (*psuche phantazomene*: *ibid.*, 8.10).

The *phantasia* of Hellenic Neoplatonists is not the creative imagination in the sense of the word's current meaning, but rather a faculty that transmits and projects reflections of higher noetic primordial principles. This faculty also translates the manifestations of archetypes into the languages of mathematics, linguistics and aesthetics. These reflections, in turn, become the paradigms of objects of the physical realm. By using analogy, imagination functions on the furthest reach of the ontological relationship between the paradigm (*paradeigma*) and the image (*eikōn*). Even though Neoplatonism does not equate the rational soul to *phantasia*, the soul contemplates the figures (the images of noetic realities), which emerge in the transitional area of imagination, and begins to self-reflect. This contemplation prepares the soul for the ascent to divinity.

In the ancient world, the active imagination was conceptualized relatively late and it functioned without critical self-reflection. The *phantasia* of antiquity, by definition, does not play the real role of imagination in regards to allegorical interpretations of scriptures, or creating metaphysical systems and fantastical cosmologies. That is because most of the concepts which came to be retrospectively attributed to the domain of sacred imagination were in ancient times recognized as the "correct" scientific approach, as accurate reflections of reality (or objects, *pragmata*), and as totally unrelated to fiction (*plasmata*).

The Neoplatonic concept of imagination was developed later, during the Renaissance and the Romantic era, when alchemical practices and the theory of magical images were interpreted by using modified terms of Hellenistic philosophy in a new historical and cultural context. Imagination needed to find a place between Christianity, which wrote off everything non-Christian as heresy, and the secular worldview, which denied the existence of metaphysics. In addition, the Catholics, Lutherans and especially Calvinists of the seventeenth century began a metaphorical crusade against the demonized imagination. According to I. P. Couliano, "The censure of the imaginary and the wholesale rejection by strict Christian circles of the culture of the phantasmic age [the Renaissance] result in a radical change in the human imagination."[36] The spirit of the Reformation defeats the spirit of the Renaissance. It means that the culture of pragmatic perception of reality (the one of the Puritans, capitalists and positivists) defeats the demonized culture of Neoplatonic theurgy, alchemy, hermetical phantasmagory and erotic magic. As Couliano states: "Later on, when the religious fervour of the Reformation is

---

36. Ioan P. Couliano, *Eros and Magic in the Renaissance*, tr. by M. Cook, foreword by M. Eliade, The University Chicago Press, Chicago and London, 1987, p. 204.

extinguished, this is all that remains: the strong contrast between the imagination (pleasure principle) and free will (reality principle) and the idea that magic autism has no *real* power."[37]

Western alchemists refer to imagination as *imaginatio vera* and equate it to a "star" within a human being (*astrum in homine*), or a transformative spiritual rudiment. Understood in such a way, imagination is not the creator of poetic or artistic substitutes for reality, but a tool for transcendental knowledge, a means to directly experience and comprehend hierarchically higher levels of being. Such a concept of imagination is based on talismanic and hieroglyphical magic, practiced by Renaissance Hermeticists. However, its roots lie in the Islamic Arabian-Persian civilization, which, in its own way, synthesized the cultural heritage of classical Antiquity and the ancient Near East. More precisely, this concept of imagination originated in the inward dimension of the above-mentioned civilization, represented by various traditions of Shi'ism, Sufism and Ismailism that adopted the ideas of Hermeticism, Gnosticism and Neoplatonism as well as the practices of Egyptian alchemy and magic, related to the sacramental powers of the Qur'an. In retrospect, even the Egyptian *Book of the Dead* strikes as a practice of imagination that creates a semiotic text of reality, intended for ritualistic transformation of the spirit.[38]

In the context of the hierarchical relationship between the archetype and the image, the vision of the external world, reflected by the imagination, are merely secondary in comparison to the images of the Ideas of the noetic cosmos. From this perspective, the image that appears in the mirror of imagination originates not from the domain of external senses (which belongs to an even lower category of reflections), but from a domain of intellectual light. If the imagination exploits such ontologically strong images, it can also meaningfully trans-

---

37. *Ibid.*, p. 221.
38. Algis Uždavinys, *Egipto mirusiųjų knyga*, Ramduva, Kaunas, 2003.

form the information of the external world by turning these images into various symbols (that can be identified in the imaginative plane of the spirit, which H. Corbin calls *mundus imaginalis*) and living mythical figures, which aid in the procedures of interpreting the reality.

The physical phenomena that are comprehended with the help of the active imagination are seemingly dematerialized and turned into spiritually transparent forms. As mentioned before, these forms precede others and are closer to the divine Intellect from the perspective of ontological hierarchy. While existing as images of higher paradigms, they themselves serve as paradigms with respect to material objects and phenomena. That is why hermeneutic imagination "returns" a phenomena to the ideal imaginative domain, as well as sees and interprets the physical reality through the prism of "the world of imagination". The Neoplatonic system of hypostases allows the construction of a cosmological structure (a transitional world of imaginative figures), accessible only by the active imagination. This metaphysical realm was conceptualized and adapted for a new spiritual mythology by the Sufis. They referred to it as the world of autonomous images or similitudes (*'ālam al-mithāl*).

Henry Corbin gives a lot of praise to this kind of Neoplatonic-Zoroastrian imagination (*khayāl*), which is acknowledged in theosophical Arabian-Persian systems and has metaphysical, alchemical and mystical functions. According to him, *imaginatio vera* is not just a tool for creating fiction—it can also help to reveal a hidden reality.[39] In other words, it reveals what ancient hermeneuts called *huponoia*, or a deep allegorical meaning.[40] However, right now this *huponoia* and its dimension of abstract philosophical meanings (in the example of the *Chaldean Oracles*) becomes a personalized "world"

---

39. Henry Corbin Spiritual, *Body and Celestial Earth, From Mazdean Iran to Shi'ite Iran*, tr. by N. Pearson, I.B. Tauris, London, 1990, p. 12.

40. Algis Uždavinys, *Hermeneutinės strategijos antikos pasaulyje. Rytai-Vakarai: kultūrų sąveika*. Logos leidykla, Vilnius, 2002, p. 82–89.

of mythical images and figures (*'ālam*) that contains both microcosmic and macrocosmic aspects. It is "the real earth" described in Plato's *Phaedo* (109a ff.), which becomes the source of cosmological visions, as well as soteriological dreams and revelations. With the help of imagination, one can enter it as if it were Osiris' Fields of Reeds or a virtual reality—much brighter, vibrant and more real than the reality of the physical world. Here, one can visit heavenly cities, meet mystical spiritual guides and prophets, and experience the effect of iconographic symbols that channel transcendent primordial principles.

Metaphysically emphasized imagination enables spiritual exegesis (*ta'wīl*) and alchemical meditation. Its provided knowledge (*gnosis, ma'rifah*) signifies that any object of the external reality is experienced not in its "objective" physical aspect, but rather as a symbol that transforms the spirit and directs it toward higher levels of spiritual consciousness. Plotinus noted that the senses, in this case, are merely vague intellections. However, as they become stronger, they automatically transport a person to the domain of noetic phenomena. This action (the Neoplatonic *epistrophê*) represents the alchemical "transformation" of the external reality, i.e. the ability to witness the outside world as a sacred image or a transparent veil through which one can see noetic archetypes. Here, living mythical figures appear. They testify that *The Divine Comedy* never ceases to take place in the Soul of the world.

· SYMBOLIC VISION AND ITS GEOGRAPHY ·

From the perspective of metaphysical imagination, a symbol is understood not as a conventional sign, but rather as ontological realia, woven into the fabric of reality. To a soul, a symbol can testify inexpressible transcendental truths. According to the *Chaldean Oracles*, the Demiurge (or the fatherly Intellection) scattered the symbols across the universe as if they were seeds, so that they would become the means of returning to the spiritual source: "For the Paternal Intellect has sown symbols throughout the cosmos, (the Intellect) which thinks the intelligibles. And (these intelligibles) are called inexpressible beauties." (fr. 108)

Some ancient Neoplatonists, like Proclus, made a clear distinction between images and symbols (usually theurgical symbols, which do not resemble the object symbolized). However, it is difficult to clearly differentiate between the categories of riddles (*ainigma*), allegories (*allegoria*) and symbols (*sumbolon*) when it comes to the times of Antiquity.

In the intellectual Islamic tradition, allegories, symbols, images and similitudes merge into a single complex of symbolic representation. The Ismailis, for example, claim that the Qur'an-based religious law (*sharī'a*) is the external (*ẓāhir*) part of the internal reality (*ḥaqīqa*). In turn, *ḥaqīqa* is an esoteric, or an internal (*bāṭin*) aspect of the religious law. In this regard, the religious law is the symbol of the inner truth.

W. Ivanow, as quoted by H. Corbin, translates the concept of *mithāl* (which can mean both an image and a similitude) as a "symbol". Additionally, he perceives *ḥaqīqa* as the Idea. Thus, the Idea is *mamthūl*—the object that is symbolized. H. Corbin explains that *mithāl* is not an allegory, but a symbol.[41] This kind of approach is rather retrospective as, in Antiquity, the concepts of allegory and symbol are often used as synonyms. However, in the Islamic civilization, the spectrum of the meanings that fall under the term *mithāl* is very wide. Only when the Baroque literature and rhetorics banalized and humanized *the allegory*, did the Romantics introduce *the symbol* as an antonym of the allegory.

In Proclus' philosophy, this contrast between the symbol and the allegory is partly expressed by the contrast between the metaphysically perceived theurgical symbol (*sumbolon*, *sunthema*) and the image (*eikon*). Here, the symbol is regarded as a god-given tool for enlightenment and mystical con-

---

41. Henry Corbin, *Avicenna and the Visionary Recital*, tr. by W. R. Trask, Bollingen Series LXVI, Princeton University Press, 1988, p. 30.

nection. This particular version of understanding the symbol becomes the basis for all the later theories that juxtapose allegories and symbols. That is why, when translating ambiguous Ismaili terms into the language of philosophy, H. Corbin emphasizes that "*Tamthīl* is not an 'allegorization', but the typification, the privileged exemplification of an archetype. *Tamaththul* is the state of the sensible or imaginable thing that possesses this investiture of the archetype, and this investiture, making it symbolize with the archetype, exalts it to its maximum meaning."[42]

The mentioned concept of the symbol is inseparable from the Neoplatonic or Neo-Aristotelian model of the structure of hierarchical existence. While this model is naively analogous to reality, talking in symbols and allegories (saying one thing while meaning another) is very similar to it. Destroying the Neoplatonic universe or the Ptolemaic cosmological scheme and replacing the realistic worldview with a nominalist one, the exegetical allegories and symbols are reduced into a single plane of conventional discourse. Thus, metaphysicians deem it important to preserve the anagogical symbol at any cost by strictly distinguishing it from conventional signs. The symbol is given a mystical polysemantic depth, which can never be fully interpreted. If a hermeneut wants to discursively define a symbol, as well as rationalize it and reveal its "literary" content, he has to turn it into an allegory, i.e. a semantic formula independent from the transcendental signifier (whose unlimited potency makes the symbol inexhaustible). In this way, the symbol loses its main function: to lift and transform the spirit by changing the identity of consciousness and to merge it with divine origins. However, such an opportunity arises only when one accepts appropriate metaphysical and ontological assumptions and their respective religious-mystical cosmological system.

According to Persian Sufis and Shia Muslims, symbolic text exegesis (*ta'wīl*) is followed by the exegesis of the soul

---

42. *Idem.*

(*ta'wil*), and that is why the inner truth of the text is perceived as the inner truth of the soul (*haqīqa*). The text of a sacred book or the cosmic reality becomes a means for transmutation, and physical objects turn into symbols. Thus, symbolic perception implies a symbolic geography of visions.

By following the example of Iranian Mazdeans, H. Corbin refers to the imaginal landscape as "the *Xvarnah* landscape". *Xvarnah* is "the Light of Glory"[43] that creates the space of sacred theophanies. According to ancient Egyptians, this sacred space is filled with the manifestations (rays of an all-creating and all-sustaining Intellect) of Ra, god of the sun, or Phat, the demiurge of Memphis. One can witness it with the help of metaphysical-alchemical imagination. Thus, the topography of the physical reality can be seen as a divine body and a map of symbolic meanings.

Similarly, in the Mazdean religion (which worships Ahura Mazda), worldly phenomena are perceived as the hierophanies of transcendental entities. These hierophanies have their own noetic origins (or the sources of *xvarnah*), as well as divine doubles that appear in the form of mythical beings. That is why metaphysical imagination depicts the symbolic image of the Earth as an angel that represents Earth's internal essence. As H. Corbin states, "the Mazdean phenomenology of the Earth is, properly speaking, an angelology."[44]

When the macrocosmic and microcosmic analogies are determined, the sacred qualities of the soul can be recognized in a person's environment, which is then modelled in the example of the ideal symbolic iconography. Imagination transforms the landscape that becomes an open dimension of the Soul of the World. In this dimension, an individual soul recognizes effective soteriological signs and the manifestations of the divine light. That is why sacred botanics and the cultivation of flowers became liturgical in Sassanid Persia.

---

43. *Ibid.*, p. 29.
44. Henry Corbin, *Spiritual Body and Celestial Earth, From Mazdean Iran to Shi'ite Iran*, tr.by N. Pearson, I.B. Tauris, London, 1990, p. 30.

Every angel of Ahura Mazda has an associated flower, perceived as a hermetic talisman or an emblem. If one wishes to witness and contemplate the figure of an angel, they must contemplate the recipient of the angel's powers—a specific flower. In this way, the flower plays the role of an Indian yantra. This kind of symbol directly testifies about divine realities. That is why, aside from liturgical functions, the art of gardening also performs theurgical functions, as the garden itself is seen as a mandala that radiates immaculate heavenly light.

The tradition of the art of gardening remained in Islamic Iran—however, Mazdean mythical figures were replaced with the terminology of Sufi metaphysics. Persian garden ponds with lotus flowers, cypress alleys and flower gardens create a special "feeling of a place" (ma'had), as such a "place" reflects the whole universe, or a bloom of hierophanies, unfurled around the central axis of divine unity. Here, all the geometrical figures, colours and fabrics have an intrinsic meaning—like in Neoplatorism and Neopythagoreanism of Late Antiquity. The garden (bagh) and its courtyard (hayat), which manifest from the central point of the mandala, correlate as the external (al-ẓāhir) and internal (al-bāṭin) areas in the Qur'anic hermeneutics.

In the terminology of Hellenistic alchemy, meditative flowers play the role of the foundational matter and can reconstruct the ideal Paradise Garden in the internal plane of the soul. These flowers are perceived as the emblems of divine beings. Thus, contemplating them awakens the energies of said beings, which, in turn, affect the contemplating soul and create a field of mental visions, where there appear the visible forms of angels and mythical inhabitants of the garden. The form-possessing bodily substance and the ideal noetic substance merge into a single symbolic universe of celestial light (nūrānī), where physical matter is dematerialized, and where incorporeal entities become corporeal or turn into living existential figures.

It seems that Origen's and Plotinus' thoughts about noetic senses arise from similar sources. Sensorially perceived matter is merely a place (*mazhar*) for the manifestation of the images, transmitted from a higher dimension of reality. Akin to a mirror, it is able to reflect light in the right circumstances, but is unable if tilted at the wrong angle or if its surface is damaged. At the same time, it is a mirror of the heart and a place for the manifestation of a deity. However, it is the meditating soul with its active alchemical imagination that awakens the divine epiphanies which, in turn, purify it and help it ascend. Thus, the soul (*nafs*) of the microcosm merges into the archetypal image of the Soul of the World, which can be compared to the mythical "Earth of Real Truth".

When contemplating the cosmological dimension of imagination, the "gardener" (this epithet also refers to the Creator of the cosmos) contemplates himself. As a seventeenth-century Iranian author Mohsen Fayz states, "This intermediate world occupies in the macrocosm the same rank as the Imagination in the microcosm."[45] Hence, *mundus imaginalis* is structured in accordance with the ontological hierarchy with the macrocosmic equivalents to all the elements and abilities of the microcosm (the human being). That is why metaphysical realism-based philosophy envisions this hypostasis of the cosmic Imagination (the section between the Nature and the Soul that reflects the Intellect) as a real "world" with its plants, animals, minerals, rivers, mountains, gardens and cities with mythical inhabitants. It is not difficult to understand that the heavenly world of Osiris with its cultivated fields, cities, rivers, islands and waterways is constructed with similar principles of magical semiotics and imagination.

In this transitional cosmological territory called the Earth of Truth, spirits are incarnated and bodies are spiritualized. According to Ibn 'Arabi, a Sufi Muslim scholar and philosopher:

---

45. *Ibid.*, p. 84.

This Earth is the place of visionary recitals, of prayer in dialogue; it is not the place of mystical annihilations, of the abysses of negative theology, but the place of divine epiphanies (*tajalliyāt ilāhiyya*). [...] Every form in which these epiphanies are clothed, as well as every form in which man sees himself in dreams or in the intermediate state between waking and sleeping, or in that state of active meditation which is a state of waking while the senses are asleep—all this belongs to the *body* of this Earth of Truth.[46]

H. Corbin states that "the active Imagination (*takhayyul*) is the mirror *par excellence*, the epiphanic place (*mazhar*) of the Images of the archetypal world."[47] Imagination not only creates this world of the Images, but also transforms the components of the physical world (as physical realities are the reflections of the realities of the Soul of the World) into symbols, i.e. it "restores" them to a higher level of reality. Such "restoration" is akin to a physical body's transmutation into a subtle body of spiritual light called "the Resurrection Body".[48] In this regard, "resurrection from the dead" means a transition to the cosmological dimension of imagination. Mystical vision allows one to experience this dimension as an alchemically transformed world of external phenomena, "returned" into its imaginal Earth of Truth.

As H. Corbin writes, it is in this place of epiphanies that "Pythagoras [...] was able to perceive the melody of the Spheres, the cosmic music—that is to say, outside of his material body and without his organs of sensory perception".[49] On an archetypal level, the sights, the light and the sounds merge into one. It is not surprising that this dramaturgy of the world of imagination justifies ritualistic practices and explains the origin of symbolic revelations.

---

46. *Ibid.*, p. 83.
47. *Ibid.*, p. 88.
48. *Ibid.*, p. 95.
49. *Ibid.*, p. 88.

· THE POWER OF FANTASTICAL GENEALOGIES ·

How does all of this relate to Hermes Trismegistus? Let us not forget that the names of Hermes and Zoroaster were often used as titles or symbolic emblems. The supposed Zoroaster (whose name might have been used to emphasize a subject's "oriental" origin) is credited for everything from the astrological doctrines of Babylonian Chaldeans to the alchemical teachings of the Hellenistic period. During the reign of the Achaemenid Empire in Egypt (559–330 BC), Thoth's wisdom tradition, as well as the traditions of the Iranians and Babylonian Chaldeans (despite the mutual animosity between the Persians and the Egyptians) all came into direct contact. Hellenism (323–31 BC), in turn, provided these traditions with new scientific cosmology, a system of cultural education (*paideia*) and the principles of logic and philosophical discourse.

Oftentimes, it is difficult to determine who adopted whose ideas, keeping in mind that the early Islamic civilization (during the times of the Umayyad dynasty and the Abbasid Caliphate) used Hermes Trismegistus (at the time referred to as the prophet Idris) to successfully Islamize a part of Hellenic philosophy and to integrate the remnants of the wisdom of ancient civilizations. This medley of various esoteric traditions, comprised of Hellenistic philosophy (Stoicism, Platonism, Aristotelianism), Hellenistic science, Hermeticism, Gnosticism and the myths and rituals of the Middle East reached Western Europe in a very fragmented and distorted form.

The union between Christianity and "natural magic" (*magia naturalis*), proposed by Renaissance thinkers, is a result of Imaginal Hermeneutics. Its nature was determined by various mythical and religious beliefs when painting a detailed picture of Biblical "history". One-sided and sometimes out of touch with reality, the Christian consciousness decided to adopt the newly-discovered Platonism (more accurately—the philosophy of Plotinus and his followers) because it had supposedly originated from the revelations of Hermes Trismegistus, who, being the avatar of God and a contemporary of Moses, preached identical or similar truths. Moses, in turn, is regarded as the founder of the secret science of Kabbalah.

This project of "perennial wisdom", started in the Renaissance, is based on symbolic genealogy. However, the latter was not only interpreted literally, but also equated to factual history. All it took was the alteration of a few historical details, and the whole metaphysical project fell apart. The situation can be explained by a vivid example. Let us say that the fate of the Roman Empire unfolds as follows: Christianity vanishes and another intolerant religion takes over. Many years pass, a group of people find a few gospels, become enthralled by them and thus announce Christ and the Evangelists as the contemporaries of their own mythical avatar (who presumably lived a few hundred years before Christ). As a result, Jesus Christ's teachings gain a lot of attention. However, some "hateful" person suddenly proves that the gospels were written not in the ancient times of, say, the Egyptian pharaoh Cheops, but rather two and a half thousand years later. That is enough to disprove the texts, so Christ and his teachings lose everyone's interest.

Unbelievable as it might sound, but that is precisely what happened in Post-Renaissance Europe, when an anti-Hermeticist philologist Isaac Casaubon "proved in 1614 (*De rebus sacris ecclesiasticis exercitationes XVI*, published in London) that the texts of the *Corpus Hermeticum* are no earlier than the first centuries of the Christian Era."[50] This "verdict" undermined the status of the *Corpus Hermeticum* in the figurative context of "wisdom history". Even though fantastical genealogies remain, it is no longer possible to attribute the book to the "first theologian" Mercury, so revered by Marsilio Ficino and Giovanni Pico della Mirandola. Genealogy appears to

---

50. Antoine Faivre, *The Eternal Hermes. From Greek God to Alchemical Magus*, tr. by Joscelyn Godwin, Phanes Press, Grand Rapids, 1995, p. 186.

be more important than metaphysical or philosophical content. We can glimpse at a few such genealogies, in which the mythical Hermes Trismegistus appears in one way or another.

To quote A. Faivre, "there are also lists of what are called the "sectaries" of Trismegistus. Maier, in *Symbola aureae*, offers us his own version,

> Mena, king of Egypt, whose tutor was Hermes Trismegistus; Busiris, who founded Heliopolis; Sesostris, who raised the great statues at Memphis in the Temple of Vulcan; Sethon, in the 3228th year of the world; Adfar Alexandrinus, who taught the art of alchemy to Morienus [...]; lastly, Calid the Saracen, an Egyptian who was the pupil of Morienus."[51]

The supporters of the Christian-Jewish mythology were unfavourable toward Hermes. According to Roger Bacon, "intellectual history began with a plenary divine revelation, of which the Patriarchs were the beneficiaries. The knowledge thus acquired declined because of the sins of humanity, the invention of magic by Zoroaster, and the corruption of wisdom in the hands of Nimrod, Atlas, Prometheus, Aesculapius, Apollo-and Hermes Trismegistus. [...] Wisdom, restored with Solomon, suffered a new decline that lasted until Thales and Aristotle put philosophy back on its feet again."[52] This kind of philosophical history can astonish even the most radical postmodernist. A. Faivre describes another genealogy:

> A text attributed by esoteric tradition to Saint Thomas Aquinas, and cited by Michael Maier, recounts how Abel, the son of Adam, wrote about the virtues and properties of the planets, but was well aware that the Deluge would happen, and so was careful to engrave his teachings on stones. Several centuries after Noah, these stones passed to Mercury Trismegistus—then to Saint Thomas himself, who used them

---

51. *Ibid.*, p. 97.
52. *Ibid.*, p. 96.

to draw up talismans, Maier's book, recalling the existence of a *Liber de secretis chymicis* attributed to Albertus Magnus, states that Alexander the Great, when visiting the Oracle of Ammon, discovered a tomb of Hermes containing a *tabula Zaradi*, that is, "smaragdine" or emerald.[53] We also learn, thanks to the *Liber de secretissimo philosopho-um opere chemico* (fifteenth century) that Hermes travelled to the Valley of Hebron, where Adam was buried, and there found seven tablets of stone written before the Deluge, containing the doctrine of the Seven Liberal Arts.[54]

A very elaborate historical vision was offered by Scribonius, writing in Marburg in 1583. He states that one should distinguish four schools of physics, i.e., of natural philosophy—a curious theory that resembles that of the four monarchies held by the historiographers of his time. Scribonius names: (A) The Assyrian School, founded by Adam, emphasizing astronomy, astrology, and the interpretation of dreams, and including Noah, Abraham, Moses, David, and Solomon. (B) The Egyptian School, taught by Abraham, in which Hermes and the Persian Magi flourished. [...] (C) The Greek School, in which he includes the Druids, the Brahmins and Gymnosophists of India, and also the astrologers and magicians of Scribonius's time who, if one is to believe the Portuguese voyagers, could still enter at will into communication with discarnate entities. (D) The Roman or Latin School, with Cicero and physicians such as Vesalius.[55]

Scribonius' classification may sound astounding—just like the following theory:

In 1684, Kriegsmann, an author who otherwise distinguished himself with a commentary on the *Emerald Tablet*, published at Tübingen a work entitled *Conjectures on the origin of the*

---

53. *Ibid.*, p. 94.
54. *Ibid.*, p. 96.
55. *Ibid.*, p. 101.

German people, and their founder Hermes Trismegistus, who is
Chanaan to Moses, Tuitus to Tacitus, and Mercury to the Gentiles.
He studies at length the evidences of Antiquity concerning
Ascenates, Tuiton, the Phoenician Taaut, the Egyptian Thoth,
and other names. His conclusion is that a Phoenician colony
came to Europe, led by Tuiton, i.e. Chanaan and Mercury
Trismegistus, or by his son Mannus, and deduces that our
Mercury was the founder of Germany.[56]

Once I. Casaubon confirmed that *Corpus Hermeticum* was
not created during the First Dynasty of ancient Egypt or in
the times of the legendary Moses, the appeal of Hermeticism
started to fade, and the mythical consciousness, obsessed
with "the search for origins", started to turn to China for inspiration. On the one hand, Hermeticism starts to change
into occult Theosophy or Masonic obscurantism of the
eighteenth century, on the other hand—an experimental
science of the early modern period. It even permeates into
Lutheranism in the form of Greek humanism. Meanwhile, in
the opinion of various Platonic intellectuals (for example, R.
Cudworth), the dating of the *Corpus Hermeticum* is completely irrelevant. The most important aspect is its metaphysical
content, not the time of creation.

Persecuted by both Calvinists and their opponents, sixteenth and seventeenth century Hermeticists tend to lean
toward physics, iatrochemistry and alchemy, the latter being emancipated from spirituality and understood literally.
Gradually, they become the pioneers of modern empirical
science—a byproduct of political-magical utopianism. Freed
from its esoteric principles and facing a despiritualized world
of post-Descartes matter (*res extensa*), empirical science finally becomes a capitalism-serving weapon of rationalism and a
tool of technocracy, hidden behind the mask of humanism.

---

56. L. Massignon, "Inventaire de la littérature hermétique arabe."
Appendix III in A. J. Festugière and A. D. Nock, *La Révélation d'Hermes*
Trismégiste, Paris, p. 384–400.

· PROPHET IDRIS IN THE ISLAMIC WORLD ·

During the early Islamic civilization, Hermes Trismegistus was referred to as the father of philosophers and sages (*Abū'l-ḥukamā'*)—the bringer of the original wisdom (*ḥikma*). The legacy of Hellenism and ancient Eastern cultures is legalized under the guise of Hermes, as his name is associated with the Qur'anic prophet Idris: "And make mention in the Scripture of Idrīs. Lo! he was a saint, a Prophet" (*wa'dhkur fi'l-kitābi Idrīs innahu kāna ṣiddīqan nabiyya*— Qur'an XIX, 56).

This mysterious prophet is regarded as the first teacher of science and philosophy. In Ibn al-Nadim's *The Catalogue* (*al-Fihrist*), it is stated that thirty scriptures were revealed to Idris—this was the third revelation to humanity. A part of these scriptures is about theurgy (*ṭalismāt*), alchemy and astrology.

The figure of prophet Idris is partly related to the Mesopotamian Enki, the ruler of the waters of the deep (*abzu*) and the god of wisdom, crafts, magic and creation. His Ugaritic counterpart is *Kothar-wa-Khasis*—"Skilful-and-Wise". Kothar is also called *Hayyan hrs yd*, which means "deft with both hands". The Phoenician word *hrs* also means *blacksmith*. Kothar is linked with Memphis—the residence (*het-ka-ptah*) of Ptah, the Egyptian demiurge and god of crafts. Ugaritic texts call him "Lord of all divine Memphis" (*b'l hkpt*), thus referring to ancient Egypt, the source of the "wisdom tradition", which unifies consecration, worship, musical liturgy, crafts and magic.

The Arabian Sayyidna Idris is the ruler of the heaven of the Sun, associated with the Jewish Enoch (*Ukhnukh*) and the Egyptian Hermes Trismegistus (whose tomb is thought to be the pyramid of Surd, built before the deluge). It is impossible to connect all the myths about the tradition of Prophet Idris into a single logical system because Hermes has become a paradigm of the scientific and philosophical imagination—a multifaceted mask of the Greek, Egyptian, Persian, Phoenician, Babylonian and Asyrian wisdom. In Persia and

Mesopotamia, Hermeticism was widespread even before Islam. According to J. Ruska and Massignon, Hermeticism was prevalent not only in the Sassanid Empire (224 to 651 AD), but also in the Achaemenid Empire since the conquest of Egypt (525 BC).[57]

Abu Ma'shar, a Persian Muslim astrologer, distinguished three separate Hermes:

> The first Hermes, identified with Idris and Enoch, was the first to have discussed 'upper things,' such as the motion of the stars, and wrote many books about terrestrial and celestial sciences. Having been instructed by his grandfather Adam, he predicted the coming of the Flood and built pyramids and temples, carving inscriptions on their walls (or, in some versions, depositing books in their interiors) in order to preserve the antediluvian sciences. The second Hermes was a Chaldean wise man who lived in Babylon and revived the sciences after the Flood; Pythagoras was his student. The third Hermes was a physician and philosopher who lived in Egypt after the Flood, wrote books, wandered through the land, and had a student named Asclepius who lived in Syria.[58]

S. H. Nasr summarizes all the knowledge about the three sages described by Abu Ma'shar:

> 1) The first Hermes or Hirmis al-harāmisa was considered by some a descendant of Gayomarth and believed he was the same as Ukhnukh and Idris. He was considered the first man to have gained a knowledge of the heavens and to have instructed people in medicine. He was believed to be the inventor of the alphabet and writing, and the teacher of the wearing of clothing to mankind. It was also he who

---

57. Daniel Stolzenberg, *Egyptian Oedipus: Athanasius Kircher and the Secrets of Antiquity*, The University of Chicago Press, Chicago, 2013, p. 155.

58. C. Burnett, "The Legend of the Three Hermes." *Journal of the Warburg and Courtauld Institutes*, XXXIX, 1976, p. 231–234.

built houses in which to worship God and foresaw the storm of Noah.

2) The second Hermes or the Babylonian Hermes, who lived in Babylon after the storm, was a master in medicine, philosophy and the science of property of numbers, and revived science and philosophy after the storm. It was he who rebuilt Babylon after Nimrod and spread science there. He was also the master of Pythagoras.

3) The third or Egyptian Hermes, who was born in Manaf near Fustat (which had been the centre of science before Alexandria) and was the student of Agathedemon. He built numerous cities, including Edessa, and made many journeys during which he established traditions for the people of each climate in accordance with their particular conditions. He wrote a book on animals and was a master in the sciences of medicine, philosophy, alchemy and the proper ties of poisons. The third Hermes devised feasts at moments of the first appearance of the crescent of the crescent of the moon, the entrance of the sun into each sign of the Zodiac and the auspicious astrological conjunctions. He left certain proverbs on the importance of science, philosophy and justice and was the master of Asclepius.[59]

To Abu Ma'shar, Hermes is a title—like Caesar or Khusrau. The name of Hermes brought the esoteric and rationalistic philosophy (the heritage of the Hellenic civilization) and authentic wisdom of the Eastern world into the Islamic culture. As Hermes is both a philosopher and a prophet, his revealed wisdom and Hellenistic science do not contradict each other. Even before Islam, Hermes was regarded as the source of wisdom and early science in the Middle East. It was not difficult to remodel this Hermetic Greek, Egyptian and Persian tradition into an Islamic tradition while appealing to the Qur'an and Arabian legends. According to Ibn al-Nadim, Hermes

---

59. Seyyed Hossein Nasr, *Hermes and Hermetic writings in the Islamic World*, SUNY Press, New York, 1981, p. 105–106.

was a sage who travelled from Babylonia to Egypt, and an Egyptian pharaoh, the first one to speak about the art of alchemy (*Fihrist* 843-844). For the Chaldeans, the Babylonian Hermes built the temple of Utarid (Mercury) because, in the Chaldean language, "Utarid is Hermes" (*ibid.*). "One of his sons was Tat (Thoth). When he died, he was buried in a pyramid at Misr."[60]

According to S. H. Nasr, "Ahmad ibn Tayyib al-Sarakhsi, the famous student of al-Kindi, considered Hermes the founder of the Sabaean religion, and wrote that his master, al-Kindi, was filled with joy when he read the 'Sermon of Hermes' to his son,"[61] which spoke about the sacred unity (*tawḥīd*), emphasizing transcendence, unattainable with syllogism. In this way, discursive logic is contrasted with theurgy, which is regarded as superior. The Hermetic tradition, regarded as the teachings of prophet Idris, gets integrated into the Islamic culture earlier than Aristotle's syllogism and metaphysics. Influenced by Hermetic ideas, the Sufis juxtaposed the mind and the spirit (*rūḥ*), claiming divine inspiration (*ilhām*) to be superior to a syllogistic way of thinking. From this point of view, Hermeticism is similar to Stoic dialectic and the empirical method of the Hippocratic school. It is not surprising that the first Arabic grammar school of Kufa indirectly continued the tradition of the Stoic Pergamon school of grammar. Arabic Hermeticism, mixed with Neopythagoreanism and Neoplatonism, is simply referred to as sacred ancient wisdom (*ḥikma ladunniyya*).

The Arabic Hermes is a solar hero. Julian the Apostate, who was the last non-Christian Roman Emperor, mentions the "Phoenician theology" in a hymn dedicated to Helios: "The inhabitants of Edessa, a place from time immemorial sacred to Helios, associate with Helios in their temples Monimos and Azizos. Iamblichus [...] says that the secret meaning to be interpreted is that Monimos is Hermes and

---

60. *Idem.*
61. *Idem.*

Azizos is Ares, the assessors (*paredroi*) of Helios who are the channel for many blessings to the region of our earth" (Or. IV., p. 413 Wright). Here, Azizos is regarded as the morning star, while Monimos—as the evening star. In Islam, Azizos became one of the epithets for Allah. According to J. Teixidor, "in the Greco-Roman period the few monuments to the Sun god erected in the Near East were dedicated by Arabs, and it is they who were responsible for the expansion of his cult."[62] Hermes-Idris can also be regarded as the equivalent of the Mesopotamian Shamash, the god of the sun, as the Islamic tradition states that Idris ascended to Heaven alive and represents the "solar" level of being.

This is how Hermes is described by Mulla Sadra:

> Know that philosophy first issued from Adam, the chosen one of God and from his progeny Seth and Hermes and from Noah because the world can never be free of a person who establishes knowledge of the unity of God and of the return [to God]. The great Hermes disseminated it [philosophy] in the climes and in the countries and explained it and gave benefit of it to the people. He is the father of philosophers and the most learned of the knowledgeable.[63]

· THE MYSTERIOUS SABIANS: PAGANS AND HANIFS ·

Harran, a major city of the Byzantine Empire and the Sasanian Empire, whose inhabitants spoke Aramaic and Greek, never accepted Christianity. This city remained faithful to the ancient traditions of Syria-Mesopotamia and Hellenic philosophy. It was in the Harranian temple of the Moon god Sin where Emperor Julian performed the rites of atonement before his fatal battle against the Persians in 363 AD.

---

62. Javier Teixidor, *The Pagan God*, Princeton, 1977, p. 49.

63. Seyyed Hossein Nasr, *Hermes and Hermetic writings in the Islamic World*, p. 106.

As stated by M. Tardieu and I. Hadot, it is claimed that in 532 AD, a group of Neoplatonists from Athens, led by Damascius, settled down in Harran. After spending a few years in Ctesiphon (the capital of the Sasanian Empire), they were able to settle in Harran, as this city was favourable toward the members of Neoplatonic Academy.[64] According to Procopius (*Bella* 2.13.7), quoted by M. Tardieu, in 549 AD, Khosrow exempted the Harranians from taxes in return for their efforts to preserve the ancient religion and to stop the spread of Christianity.[65] Contrary to the opinion of D. Chwolson and W. Scott, M. Tardieu states that the doctrines of the Harranian Sabians are Neoplatonic instead of Hermetic. It is possible that Simplicius wrote some of his commentaries on Aristotle and Epictetus in Harran.

After the Arabs conquered Harran (633–643 AD), the situation there did not change that much. According to a popular legend, in 830 AD, an Abbasid caliph Al-Ma'mun, while on his way from Baghdad to the Byzantine Empire, visited Harran. Surprised by the customs of the Harranians, the caliph supposedly asked them, which Qur'an-approved religion they follow. The citizens answered that they are neither Christians, nor Jews or Zoroastrians, but Harranians. However, they could not answer the question whether they possessed a holy scripture and a prophet. Then, al-Ma'mun threatened to annihilate the Harranians if they did not become Muslims or followers of one of the other monotheistic religion mentioned in the Qur'an. With the help of one Muslim jurist, the Harranians prepared a suitable answer. When the caliph was traveling back from the journey (even though, in actuality, he never returned to Harran), they claimed to be Sabians, using this name mentioned in the Qur'an as a cover.

---

64. Ilsetraut Hadot, "The Life and Work of Simplicius in Greek and Arabic Sources", in *Aristotle Transformed. The Ancient Commentators and their Influence*, ed. R. Sorabji, Cornell University Press, Ithaca, 1990, p. 275–303.

65. Michel Tardieu, "Sabiens coraniques et "Sabiens" de Harran", *Journal Asiatique*, 274, 1986, p. 23.

According to D. S. Margoliouth, "the link between Harran and the Sabians had been established at least seventy-five years prior to Ma'mun's visit."[66]

It is difficult to say who the real Sabians of the Qur'an are (Qur'an 2, 59; 5, 73; 22, 17)—probably, Mandeans or the Mesopotamian Gnostics. In any case, the name of the Sabians suited the Harranians well. They also began claiming that Hermes, or Idris, was their prophet (or one of their prophets), and that the Hermetic treatises were their holy scriptures. As written by S. H. Nasr, "Thabit ibn Qurra, one of the most famous scientists of Harran, translated the *Kitāb al-nawāmis* of Hermes from Syriac into Arabic."[67] Al-Kindi's student, Ahmad ibn Tayyib al-Sarakhsi, even regarded Hermes as the founder of the Sabian religion.

In Islamic civilizations, it often occurs that all "pagans"— the members of ancient religions—are referred to as Sabians. Even the Prophet Muhammad was called *ṣābi'* by his enemies. According to Ibn Hazm, Prophet Ibrahim (Abraham) converted the Harranian Sabians to the Hanif religion. The Qur'an refers to both Abraham (3, 67) and Muhammad (16.124; 22.77) as *ḥanīf*. According to T. M. Green:

> Ibn Hazm is making the connection between Abraham and the Sabians according to a generic definition of pre-Islamic religion when he describes the Sabians in the following way: the Sabians believe in two eternal elements; they honour the seven planets and the twelve constellations, and paint them in their temples; they have five prayers similar to the Muslim ceremony, fast in Ramadan, turn to the Ka'bah in prayer and regard the same meats as unlawful as do the Muslims.[68]

---

66. Tamara M. Green, *The City of the Moon God. Religious Traditions of Harran*, E. J. Brill, Leiden, 1992, p. 106.

67. Seyyed Hossein Nasr, *Islamic Life and Thought*, SUNY Press, New York, 1981, p. 114.

68. *Ibid.*, p. 107.

This Ibn Hazm's theory explains the close connection between the Sabians and the Hanifs in the early period of Islam, the latter being the members of the original religion. As the Prophet Muhammad is also a *ṣābi'*, the first Muslims are sometimes called *ṣābi'a*. In addition, *ṣābi'* is a synonym of the word *gnostic* in a general sense. Muslim authors associated Sabians not only with the Abrahamic religions, but also with the religion of ancient Egypt, which, in their opinion, was practiced by both Hermes and Agathodaemon. Thus, it comes as no surprise that Sabian pilgrims (as is believed by Muslims) visit the Pyramids to perform their secret rituals. According to J. Hjärpe, it is non-Muslim Gnostics who are referred to as Sabians, and that the real Muslim Gnostics—or the original monotheists who lived before the Prophet Muhammad—are called Hanifs.[69]

It is possible that the word *ṣābi'* is derived from the verb *ṣb'*, which means "to want", i.e. to desire sacred knowledge. In this way, *ṣābi'* is an equivalent of a sacred thirst for knowledge of a Sufi student (*murīd*), meaning a seeker of wisdom. The term *hanpa* (the bringer of the ancient wisdom tradition, a pagan), used by Thabit ibn Qurra, is also a Syrian equivalent of the word *ḥanīf*, and it is the true source of the Arabic term. Claiming that "this blessed city [of Harran] has never been defiled with the error of Nazareth [i.e. Christianity]", Thabit ibn Qurra states: "We are the heirs and transmitters of *hanputho* [...] Lucky is he who bears the burden with a sure hope for the sake of *hanputho*." (Bar Hebraeus, *Chronography* 153). In this case, *hanputho* (the Hanifian religion, wisdom, culture and civilization in general) means both the Hellenic tradition and the tradition of Hellenized ancient Near East, as well as Neoplatonic philosophy and the teachings of Hermes Trismegistus.

---

69. J. Hjärpe, *Analyse critique des traditions arabes sur les Sabéens Harrāniens*, Uppsala, 1972, p. 24.

According to al-Masudi, an Arab historian and travel-ler who visited Harran in 943 AD, there exist a few different kinds of Sabians:

1. The kings of Rum who were *al-ḥunafā'* and *al-ṣābi'ūn* before they became Christians. The emperor Julian was secretly a Sabian, and when he renounced Christianity, he re-erect-ed the statues which the Sabians put up as images of the highest substances and the celestial bodies, and punished those who did not return to the faith of the *ḥanīfs*.
2. The Egyptian Sabians, who honour Hermes and the Agathodaimon as their prophets; the remnants of these Sabians are the Harranians. "They abstain from many foods that the Greek Sabians (i.e., those mentioned above) eat, such as pork, chicken, garlic, beans and other things of this type; they regard as their prophets Agathodaimon, Hermes, Homer, Aratus, Aryasis, Arani, the first and sec-ond of this name."
3. The followers of Zaradrusht (Zoroaster), who formerly had embraced the creed of the *ḥanīfs*.[70]

It might be difficult to understand what is meant when dis-cussing "Sabians", especially when every Muslim author proposes a separate version full of most fantastical details. However, one must not forget that these imaginal perspec-tives (totally opposite to historical positivism), or semiotic models of "memory", formed the actual horizon of cultural self-perception. This is how al-Biruni presents his classifica-tion of Sabians:

1. The real Sabians are the remnants of those Jews whom Nebuchadnezzar had transported from Jerusalem to Baby-lon and who chose to remain there. [...] Genealogically they trace themselves back to Enoch, the son of Seth, the son of Adam.

---

70. Tamara M. Green, *The City of the Moon God*, p. 115.

2. The name is also applied to the Harranians, who are the remnants of the ancient religion of the west before it converted to Christianity. They derive their system from "Aghadhimun (Agathodaimon), Hermes, Walis, Sawar. They believe that these men and other sages like them were prophets." Although they themselves did not adopt this name before AH 228 in order to be considered "among those from whom the duty of dhimma are accepted, they are better known by this name than the true Sabians. But before this time they were called hanifs, idolators and Harranians."[71]

In addition, al-Biruni claims that "the Indian Budhasaf (Buddha) called people to the religion of the Sabians. The creed was adopted by the Persian rulers of Balkh. [...] The remnants of those Sabians are living in Harran."[72]

Here, the Romans, Greek philosophers and Afghan Buddhists fall into the same category. Also, al-Biruni's reference to Balkh is not accidental (even if it seems unusual from the first glance), as the Barmakids—a dynasty of viziers and advisers, exalted by the caliph Harun al-Rashid—originated in Balkh. They were known to sponsor translations from Indian, Persian and Greek into Arabic. Before their conversion to Islam, the Barmakids are said to have supervised the Buddhist stupas in Afghanistan. It seems that they sympathized with Hermeticism, whether openly or secretly. They might have tried to cover Buddhism with the mask of the Qur'anic "Sabians" to ensure at least minimal protection. Thus, Hermes became Budhasaf (Buddha).

There is some evidence that the Parthian nobility were familiar with Hermetic teachings during the reign of the Arsacid dynasty, i.e. before the emergence of the Sassanid Empire. T. M. Green writes about "Bar Daysan of Edessa (154–222 CE), whose biography reflects the eclectic quality

---

71. *Ibid.*, p. 116.
72. *Ibid.*, p. 137.

of intellectual and religious life in Late Antiquity. He is said variously to have been educated in the Edessan royal court with the future king Abgar the Great, where, in the traditions of the Parthian nobility, he learned to excel in archery, or to have received his training at Hierapolis, from a priest who instructed him in the esoteric knowledge of the pagan traditions."[73] Later, he himself became a propagator of the Hermetic tradition: "It is reported by Ephrem [the Syrian] that he founded his own sect whose members gathered in caves to sing psalms and study texts. According to Ibn al-Nadim, who claimed that there were still scattered communities in China and Khurasan, Bar Daysan's followers had been settled in the marshlands between Wasit and Basra."[74] According to various Islamic sources, Greece is the source of Bar Daysan's ideas. He also presumably sent his sons to various schools of Athens. Bar Daysan's followers are also called Sabians.

Another Muslim author, al-Dimashqi, "posited two different kinds of Sabians: those who acknowledge the cult of the celestial mansions (i.e., worship the stars), and those who believe in idols. The former asserted that they had acquired this doctrine from Agathadaimon or Seth the prophet, the son of Adam. In fact, he suggests that they derived their name from Sabi, a son of Hermes 'who is Idris.'"[75]

· THE HARRANIAN SABIANS AND THE HELLENIC HERITAGE ·

A group of Islamic philosophers who called themselves the Brethren of Purity (*Ikhwān al-ṣafā'*) were Ismailis who systematized the Hellenic heritage. Based in Basra, Iraq (8th–10th century), they wrote numerous treatises concerning philosophy, theology, magic, mathematics, music, logic, botany and

---

73. *Ibid.*, p. 88.
74. *Ibid.*, p. 102.
75. *Ibid.*, p. 117.

mineralogy. They never revealed their real names, however, they openly stated that their philosophy came from Harranian sages, and the latter were unambiguously identified with ancient Greeks. According to Y. Marquet, these Greeks were referred to by various names, including Sabians, Harranians and Hanifs.[76]

According to the Brethren of Purity, the founder of their wisdom tradition was Pythagoras, whom they imagined as a monotheist from Harran. The Brethren of Purity also claimed that Hellenic science stemmed from Syrian and Egyptian sources (Ep. IV.295), and this genealogy reflected the Hermetic tradition, brought by the Greeks from Hellenistic Alexandria into northern Mesopotamia. Thus, it is no wonder that Agathodaemon, Hermes, Homer and Aratus are mentioned as the founders of the wisdom tradition of the Harranian Sabians (the latter is a historical figure who wrote a poem about celestial bodies called *Phaenomena* and prepared an edition of Homer's *Odyssey*).

By the example of his teacher al-Kindi, Ahmad ibn al-Tayyib refers to Hermes, Agathodaemon and Arani as the teachers of the Harranians. He adds that sometimes, "Solon, the ancestor of the philosopher Plato on his mother's side"[77] is also mentioned as one of the teachers. T. M. Green speculates that this esoteric version of the history of Greek philosophy might have been the Harranians' way of explaining the origin of their teachings. As al-Biruni states, "They have many prophets, most of whom were Greek philosophers: Hermes the Egyptian, Agathadhimun, Walis, Pythagoras, Baba, and Sw'r, the grandfather of Plato on the mother's side, and others."[78] Al-Biruni refers to Walis as a Greek philosopher who lived in Harran and was a teacher of Zoroaster. Ibn al-Adim, an Arab

76. Y. Marquet, "Sabeens et Ihwan al-Safa". *Studia Islamica* 24, 1966, p. 35–80; 25, 1966, p. 77–109.
77. Tamara M. Green, *The City of the Moon God*. Religious Traditions of Harran, p. 171.
78. *Idem.*

historian and geographer, mentions Baba as a Harranian author of prophetic books who predicted that "the might of the people of Harran will be raised to the highest degree". His predictions are included in a collection called *Prophecies of the Pagan Philosophers*, which includes predictions by Orpheus, Hermes Trismegistus, Plato and Pythagoras.[79]

Some Arab sources refer to Harranians as Greek Sabians, however, al-Masudi considers them to be the descendants of Egyptian Sabians. The word *ṣābi'ūn* can mean "Gnostics" or the original "pagans" in a general sense, yet the Harranian doctrines, described by al-Masudi and al-Biruni, do not belong to Gnosticism. Instead, they belong to Hermeticism, deeply influenced by Neopythagorean and Neoplatonist teachings, which compare Hermes to Orpheus. Some Arab authors made a clear distinction between 1) social Harranian cults and 2) an esoteric school of philosophy that preserved the remains of Hellenic wisdom and science.

According to al-Dimashqi, Harranian Sabians researched the cosmic symbolism of geometric shapes, emphasizing the esoteric meaning of the dimensions of the Pyramids. They thought that the two largest Pyramids of Giza were the tombs of Agathodaemon and Sabi, the son of Hermes. Thus, they visited them as pilgrims. They practiced alchemy, which was later adopted by Muslims. The Barmakids propagated alchemy in the palace of caliph Harun al-Rashid in Baghdad. The Hermetic alchemical tradition was continued by Jabir ibn Hayyan, who based his knowledge on a work on alchemy, attributed to Apollonius of Tyana. In his writings, he mentions a meeting, during which Hermes, Pythagoras, Socrates, Aristotle and Democritus discussed the mysteries of this science. Neither the Harrarians nor the Arab Muslims understood the chronology of Hellenic philosophy and could no longer distinguish mythical figures from historical ones, putting all of them into a single phantasmagorical mosaic, which played the role of a symbolic icon.

---

79. *Ibid.*, p. 172.

It seems that in Harran, like in all the other cities of the Caliphate, there existed closed or entirely secret craftsmen guilds that preserved the ritualistic traditions of Syrian and Mesopotamian alchemists. Later, these guilds merged with Sufism. The alchemists of Jabir's school based their wisdom on works attributed to Hermes. One of them even called Hermes the founder of alchemy. Meanwhile, the mentioned work by Apollonius of Tyana (*Sirr al-khāliqa*), according to Arabs, was discovered beneath the statue of Hermes in Tiana together with the famous Emerald Tablets (*Tabula Smaragdina*).[80] All the treatises collected or written by Jabir ibn Hayyan and his followers (including *Ghāyat al-ḥakīm*, or *Picatrix*, and *Falāḥat al-nabatiyya*, or *Nabatean Agriculture*) appear to be influenced by Babylonian Chaldeans, ancient Egyptians, Hellenic Neoplatonism, even Indian philosophy—however, Hermeticism (together with the philosophy and theurgy of Harranian Sabians) still remains the foundation of these treatises.

According to Abu Yusuf Isha' al-Qatiy'i, during the reign of Harun al-Rashid (786–809), the Harranians were referred to as the worshippers, or the followers, of the Head (*al-ra's*). As Ibn al-Nadim stated, this Head was actually a human head that resembled Utarid (Mercury)—in other words, it was a portrayal of a planet. The following Ibn al-Nadim's story may seem unbelievable, however, it most probably should not be understood in a literal sense: a man was tied up and placed into a container filled with oil and borax, in which the body became so soft that the head could be easily pulled away when the planet of Mercury reached the highest point in the sky. This procedure was repeated every year with the belief that the head contained a soul that was able to prophesize and answer questions (*Fihrist* 753ff.). It can be regarded as an equivalent to the prophetic head of Orpheus. Al-Dimashqi describes a similar prophesying head related to the planet of

---

80. Seyyed Hossein Nasr, *Islamic Life and Thought*, p. 107.

Mars, while the *Ghāyat al-ḥakīm* gives us two descriptions on how decapitated heads are able to prophesy.[81]

Ibn-al Nadim mentions a book by Harranian Sabians (*al-Hatifi*) that contains not only the instructions on how to prepare a prophetic head, but also various incantations, ritualistic chants, as well as descriptions of magical knots and talismans. As the image of a decapitated head is closely connected to the alchemic discourse, which operates on esoteric symbols and is related to the visions of an Egyptian alchemist Zosimos, we can presume that the horrific ritual, described by Ibn al-Nadim, is actually a literal interpretation of an imaginal icon, taken from a symbolic dictionary of initiation rites and related to the theurgical art of the "revival" of statues. According to a Byzantine author M. Psellos and other sources of Antiquity, Julianus the Theurgist, who led the army of Marcus Aurelius against the barbarians in 173, created a clay human head that could throw lightning, and it saved the Roman army from destruction (Psellus, *Script. Min.* I.446.28; Suidas, *s.v. Ioulianos*). The head of a statue is regarded as a mediator of daemonic or divine powers that performs theurgical and magical functions.

Through Harrarian Sabians, the Islamic Arab civilisation passed on various adapted Hermetic doctrines, Neopythagorean philosophy and Neoplatonism. This heritage of "ancient wisdom" played a major role in developing Islamic science and it especially affected Sufism. Abd al-Kahir ibn Tahir al-Baghdadi directly linked the emergence of the Islamic Batiniyya with the Harranian Sabians. He stated that both the Sabians and Batiniyya hid their teachings.[82] As already mentioned, in the Islamic world, Hermes was identified as the Qur'anic Idris and Adam's grandson Enoch, thus becoming the founder of philosophy (*falsafah*), wisdom or Gnostic knowledge (*ḥikmah*), as well as all the arts and scienc-

---

81. Tamara M. Green, *The City of the Moon God*. Religious Traditions of Harran, p. 179.
82. *Ibid.*, p. 170.

es. According to al-Masudi, the source of this identification is the Harranian Sabians (*Murūj al-dhahab* 31). Some researchers claim that the mentioned identification was approved in the middle of the ninth century or even earlier.

According to al-Farabi and al-Masudi, the "Harranian" philosophy of Hellenes-Sabians reached Baghdad in the beginning of the tenth century; however, the first link of this chain is not Athens (as is claimed by M. Tardieu as he speaks of the journey of Damascius, Simplicius, Priscian and other Neoplatonists to Ctesiphon in 529, when Christians banned philosophical teachings) but Alexandria. However, there is a huge time gap between the Neoplatonists' flight to the East and the displacement of the School of Alexandria firstly to Antiochia, and then to Harran in the middle of the eighth century. These are two separate events. The first one took place during the peak of Late Neoplatonism, which was promoted in the Academy of Athens (about fifty years after the death of Proclus), while the second one took place during the reign of Arabs. At the time of the reign of caliph al-Mutawakkil (847–861), more than a century after the death of the Prophet Muhammad, the last members of so-called "School of Alexandria" (the term here is used very loosely) moved from Alexandria to Harran.

J. Lameer states that the information about all these relocations is false and that it is based on the fantasies of Abu Nasr al-Farabi and other Arab authors. In his work *Kitab al-tanbīh wa'l-ishrāf* (955–956) al Masudi states that the Academy was relocated from Athens to Alexandria as, during the reign of Emperor Theodosius, philosophy was taught only in Alexandria. However, when Umar ibn Abd al-Aziz was in power (717–720), the Academy was relocated to Antiochia, and later, during the rule of al-Mutawakkil (847–861)—to Harran. During the reign of either al-Mu'tadid (892–902) or al-Muqtadir (908–932), the ideas of this school reached Baghdad. Al-Masudi compares Hellenic philosophy with the so-called Academy of Alexandria. J. Lameer attempts to disprove this chain by stating that the Hellenic heritage most probably was gradually adopted from Syria. In his opinion, it is unlikely that the School of Alexandria survived until the times of caliph Umar ibn Abd al-Aziz (717–720). He does not agree with the Arabic sources. which claim that Abd al-Malik ibn Abjar al-Kinani, the doctor of caliph Umar's palace, led the Academy of Alexandria at that time.[83] J. Lameer tries to find out why Antiochia and Harran were chosen as parts of this fictitious chain. However, his arguments do not appear to be very convincing, thus there is no reason to think that M. Tardieu or I. Hadot are less correct than all-doubting sceptics.

During the reign of the last Umayyad caliph Marwan II, the city of Harran briefly became the capital of the whole caliphate, however, this fact did not make the Harranians reject their ancient beliefs (*hanputho*). In his work *Chronography*, a Christian author Bar Hebraeus remarks that, a few years before caliph al-Ma'mun's arrival to Harran (830), his uncle Ibrahim, a ruler of Harran, was so tolerant that he let pagans publicly organize religious mysteries. A procession with singers and flutists together with an ox wearing a crown and covered in flowers could freely parade on the streets around the marketplace (*Chronograph.* 139).

Around the year 900, three Harranian teachers (Quwayri, Yuhanna ibn Haylan and Abu Yahya al-Marwazi) started to discuss and teach Aristotelian logic in Baghdad. According to al-Masudi, these were the Christian students of the Alexandrian philosophers who moved to Harran. However, the true Harranian Sabians—the followers of Hermes, Homer, Orpheus and Plato—did not accept Christianity.

The Sabians greatly contributed in translating Greek and Syrian texts into Arabic. One of the most famous scientists of that time, Thabit ibn Qurra, who was well-versed in Greek

---

83. Joep Lameer, "From Alexandria to Baghdad: Reflections on the Genesis of a Problematic Tradition", in *The Ancient Tradition in Christian and Islamic Hellenism. Studies on the transmission of Greek Philosophy and Sciences*, ed. Gerhard Endress and Remke Kruk, Research School CNWS, Leiden, 1997, p. 185.

and familiar with the Hellenic philosophical tradition, translated the texts, ascribed to Hermes (*Kitāb al-nawāmis*), from Syriac to Arabic. This intellectual environment associated Neoplatonism with the name of mythologized Aristotle, not only with mythical prophets. As soon as the figure of Aristotle became the archetypal mask of the whole Hellenic philosophy, there emerged an Arabic version of Plotinus' *The Enneads*, called *Aristotelian Theology*. Some people believed that Aristotle claimed that talismanic science was more accurate than geometry and more profound than philosophy (*De imaginibus*).[84]

It is possible that fragments of Greek Hermetic texts, preserved by Harranian Sabians, reached the Byzantine Empire during the so-called "Platonic Renaissance" and later appeared in Florence as *Corpus Hermeticum*.

· THE CHARACTERISTICS OF ARABIC HERMETICISM ·

S. H. Nasr accurately describes the relation between Islam and Hermeticism:

> In the Muslim world Hermeticism must be considered one of the most important factors in the construction of the Islamic view of the Universe. Its mark on both Islamic philosophy and science was a permanent one; it even entered into religious and metaphysical speculation as well as into Arabic and Persian poetry and prose. The figure of Hermes came to be regarded as that of the first teacher in science and philosophy, and through him it became possible for Muslims to integrate Greek science and philosophy into their world view without feeling that they were going anyway outside the Abrahamic prophetic tradition.[85]

---

84. *The Astronomical Works of Thabit ibn Qurra*, ed. F. J. Carmody, Berkeley, 1960, p. 180.

85. Seyyed Hossein Nasr, *Islamic Life and Thought*, p. 111–112.

In *The Catalogue* (*Kitāb al-Fihrist*), Ibn al-Nadim names twenty-two treatises by Hermes translated into Arabic. Though some of them have survived, not much is known about them as they are available only to a small group of researches. Nevertheless, these are not the only texts ascribed to Hermes available in Arabic.

A number of Shia Muslim groups partly accepted the Hermetic teachings of the Harranian Sabians. However, some of them converted to Islam and joined the newly-formed Sufi fraternities when the spiritual leader of the Sabians, Hakim ibn Isa ibn Marwan, passed away, and when Muslims started to persecute Sabians. The direct influence of Hermeticism weakened, however, this tradition survived in the form of alchemy, astrology and Hippocratic medicine. According to S. H. Nasr, "for example, belief that there is no distinction between the Divine Qualities and Names and His Essence, a characteristic of Hermetic teachings, is seen in the pseudo-Empedoclean corpus, and [...] it was influential in the doctrines of al-'Allaf, the famous Mu'tazilite theologian, and Ibn Masarrah, the Andalusian ascetic and sage."[86]

Dhul-Nun the Egyptian (Dhu'l-Nun al-Misri), an alchemist and a Sufi, introduced the School of Sufism to the idea that Aristotle's syllogisms are insufficient to reveal the metaphysical truth or to grant spiritual knowledge (*gnosis*). These ideas strongly affected Mansur al-Hallaj, a famous Sufi mystic. Hermetic cosmology (with various elements of Neoplatonism) was integrated into Islamic mysticism by Ibn Arabi, who masked it behind Qur'anic terminology, while certain symbols and ideas of the Hermetic science were adopted by esoteric Ismailism (Hamid al-Din al-Kirmani) and al-Suhrawardi's School of Illumination.

Al-Suhrawardi (who was presumably executed in 1191 in Aleppo) considered himself a member of the Hermetic tradition. He did not see any difference between Hermeticism, Pythagoreanism, Neoplatonism, Pre-Socratic philosophy

---

86. *Ibid.*, p. 108.

and Sufism as expressed by modern academic terms, as they not only "modernize", but also distort the image of historical development—sometimes even to a higher degree than the fantastical genealogies of Arabic and Greek thinkers, which first and foremost bear a symbolic meaning and play the role of initiation in the context of spiritual practice (which also includes imagination). Even though al-Suhrawardi, just like the whole tradition of Sufism and Islamic philosophy from the Umayyad era to the nineteenth century, confuses Plotinus with Aristotle, describing the latter as a Neoplatonist, he juxtaposes Aristotle's logic with the philosophy of Illumination.

Al-Razi, a Persian doctor and alchemist who lived a few centuries before al-Suhrarawardi, also criticized Aristotle for deviating from the traditions of Pythagoras and Empedocles. He even blamed Aristotle for the corruption of philosophy in general. The same ideas were held by Numenius, a Neopythagorean from Syria, and certain Neoplatonists, even though many of them compared Aristotle's philosophy to the "Lesser Mysteries".

Even during the Arab conquest, Hermetic philosophy and alchemy secretly prospered in Egypt, especially in the city of Akhmim (the former Panopolis), where a famous alchemist Zosimos once lived. When explaining the genealogy of "perennial philosophy", al-Suhrawardi refers to Dhu'l-Nun the Egyptian as "the brother of Akhmim", who passed on this wisdom to Sahl al-Tustari and his Iranian followers. Both persons mentioned are famous Sufis. Al-Suhrawardi describes Dhu'l-Nun's wisdom as "Pythagorean leaven" (*khamīrat al-fithāghūriyyīn*). A little later (9th–10th century), Ibn Suwayd, an alchemist from Akhmim, writes not only a book to advocate for Dhu'l-Nun al-Misri, but also an alchemical work called *Mushaf al-jama'a*, which becomes a prototype for the Latin *Turba philosophorum*. With the help of such treatises like Ibn Suwayd's "Book of the Red Sulphur" (*Kitāb al-kibrīt al-ahmar*), Hermetic alchemy gets integrated into Sufism, and alchemical imagery enters the vocabulary of Sufi symbolism.

ARCHETYPAL AND HISTORICAL FORMS

While recognizing the immanent aspect of divinity (as well as the analogy between microcosm and macrocosm), Hermeticism preaches about "the absolute transcendence of the Deity and the impossibility of human reason to reach knowledge of It through its own powers," as stated by S. H. Nasr. "The only path to the knowledge of the Divine is self-purification, which finally leads to illumination of the soul and the spiritual vision of the Truth. This view is similar to that of Sufism."[87] In this context, an important role is played by a sacred father, or a guide—both spiritual and secular (the latter can be regarded as the personification of the sacred Intellect). The idea of saving souls through "a saviour figure descending into this world as a 'help' (*boetheia*)" was adopted into Sufism from Manichaeism and Hermeticism. According to P. Kingsley, Empedocles (whose teachings—a distinct version of Neoplatonism—were followed by certain Sufis) is also referred to as "the helper of souls" (*ghiyāth*). *Ghiyāth al-nufūs*, a technical term of Persian Sufism that means "help of souls", originates from similar sources.[88]

The sacred guide of souls, who reminds of an inner daemon or a figure that appears in both dreams and reality in the form of a mythical teacher, is labelled by the Sufis as the "celestial witness" (*al-shahīd fī'l-samā'*), or "Perfect Nature". This "Perfect Nature" is also discussed by al-Suhrawardi, who refers to it as the celestial father and the spiritual son. In his work *al-Mutarahat*, al-Suhrawardi writes: "Hermes said I met a spiritual being who conveyed to me the science of things. I asked him who art thou? He said I am thy Perfect Nature."[89]

In Hermeticism, the "Perfect Nature" is a celestial counterpart of the soul. It is the soul's living spiritual archetype that can become a mythical and mystagogical figure with

---

87. *Ibid.*, p. 109.
88. Peter Kingsley, *Ancient Philosophy, Mystery, and Magic. Empedocles and Pythagorean Tradition*, Clarendon Press, Oxford, 1995, p. 383.
89. Seyyed Hossein Nasr, *Islamic Life and Thought*, p. 109.

the ability to appear not only as a dream, but also as a physical form, like a simulacrum that cannot be distinguished from material phenomena. On the other hand, this "Perfect Nature" is similar to the higher part of the soul described by Plotinus, the one that does not descend to the perceptible realm but remains in the heavens instead. To remember this part of the soul and to merge with it means to achieve a primordial spiritual fulfilment.

Zoroastrian angelology also depicts a perfect celestial counterpart. It states that the celestial part of the soul (*Daena*) manifests as a beautiful woman, which shows that Hermeticism and Zoroastrianism share common traits. This convergence might have occurred during the times of the Sasanian Empire. The esoteric Arab tradition adopts certain teachings on how the higher reality of a person can spiritually guide them. That is why in *Ghāyat al-ḥakīm*, or *Picatrix*, Hermes not only describes the "Perfect Nature" as the radiant source of the physical environment, compiled of four fundamental qualities—heat, cold, moisture and dryness—but he himself is also referred to as the Perfect Nature.

The Hermetic science did not agree with the Aristotelian division of the cosmos into two radically different areas of heaven and earth. Quite the opposite—it searched for analogies between different levels of being, elements, forms, colours and sounds. Nevertheless, Aristotelianism and Hermeticism are often merged into a unified synthetic philosophy of nature. Aristotelianism emphasized general reasons, while Hermeticism dealt with individual and concrete reasons. That is why the grammarians of Kufa, who based their ideas on the logic of the stoics of the school of Pergamon, were associated with Hermeticism, while the grammarians of Basra continued the tradition of the Peripatetics of Alexandria. In the Arabic world, experimental methods of Hermeticism and the science of spiritual alchemy were always closely connected with the school of Hippocrates, which addressed both bodily and spiritual health from the perspective of a living cosmos. In the meantime, many Arab authors emphasized the connection between Ishraqi philosophy and the Hermetic Egyptian tradition. One of them was Ibn Wahshiyya, who wrote that the Ishraqi followers of al-Suhrawardi were the descendants of the sister of Hermes.[90]

90. *Ibid.*, p. 116.

CHAPTER 2

THE EGYPTIAN GOD THOTH
AND THE HERMETIC TRADITION

· HERMES AS A HERMENEUT AND THE GUIDE OF SOULS ·

The hermeneutic tradition, which draws comparison between various gods of different cultures, was born in the Akkadian Empire. This tradition of cosmopolitan metaphysics is based on the idea that, from the perspective of sacred reality, there exists only a single religion, and that different cultures and civilizations worship identical gods but refer to them by different names. The presence of sacred vibrations and theophanies disguises the unity and homogenous essence of fundamental principles. That is why any theological system can be conveyed by the terminology of another theological system. Translation is a possible and natural occurrence despite the distinctiveness that constitutes the original and unique nature of each individual religion.

At the time of Hellenism, the hermeneutics of sacred names became the universal paradigm of the civilized world and guaranteed mutual understanding and tolerance. Cosmic phenomena and sacred manifestations hide universal and transcendental principles, which do not belong to a single confession of faith. Civilized people of the past believed that the same gods were worshipped by the Hellenes, Egyptians, Phoenicians, Indians, Ethiopians, Chaldeans, Arabs and other nations. They were only given different forms, names, and iconographic depictions.

This harmony of traditional polytheism was merciless-
ly dismantled by the traditions of semitic monotheism, to
which J. Assmann appropriately refers as "contra-religions".[1]
This exegesis of sacred names, based on the cosmogonic dialectic between the One and the Many, had a universal status—however, it was placed into the domain of esoterics and
speculations by monotheistic religions. A deeper metaphysical awareness (or Neoplatonic Hermeneutics) becomes secret
knowledge, which is interpreted as the "real" or the "inner"
meaning of the official monotheistic doctrine.

To this day, many researchers cannot understand how
Hermes, the Greek trickster and thief, could be seen as
Thoth—the lord of the all-creating Word and the inventor of
hieroglyphs (that are akin to the Platonic forms), responsible for maintaining the eternal order (*maat*). So, what are the
most important traits of the Hellenic Hermes? It is a trickster of many different looks, who protects borders and crossroads. As a result, a monument that marks the borders of a
certain territory is called a herma. According to W. Burkert,
the Mycenaean culture personified the protective power of
such monuments as *Herma-as* or *Herma-on*, while the Dorians
had *Herman*. The Ionians built pillars that featured a head of
a bearded man and an erect phallus. Such a geometricized
monument, reminiscent of the Egyptian god Min, is called
Hermes.[2]

Hermes the Olympian is also an inventor, the creator of
civilization and the messenger of the gods. The latter concept might be inspired by the epic poetry of the Middle
East. However, Hermes not only protects the boundaries—
he also breaks them. That is why this god is the patron of
shepherds and thieves, the bringer of news and the overseer
of graveyards, which represent the crossroad between this

1. Jan Assmann, *Moses the Egyptian. The Memory of Egypt in Western
Monotheism*, Harvard University Press, Cambridge, MA, 2002, p. 3–7.

2. Walter Burkert, *Greek Religion*, tr. by John Raffan, Harvard University
Press, Cambridge, MA, 1985, p. 156.

world and the afterlife. As a psychopomp, chthonic Hermes guides souls into the world of the dead. In mythical Egyptian theology, this function is performed by Upuaut ("Opener of the Ways") and Anubis—that is why, during the reign of the Roman Empire, Hermes is merged with Anubis, thus becoming Hermanubis.

According to Hellenic myths, which reflect the doctrines of archaic cosmogony, after stealing Apollo's cattle, Hermes invents the lyre from a shell of a tortoise and gives it to Apollo. In addition, Hermes is said to be the inventor of fire and sacrifice. With the help of his caduceus (possibly inspired by the Egyptian staff), Hermes puts to sleep Argus, the many-eyed giant who guards Io, a priestess of the Goddess Hera, who later reaches Egypt in the form of a cow. During the times of Hellenism, Io is regarded as the hypostasis of Isis. Two mating snakes are entwined around Hermes' caduceus, symbolizing mental powers. These snakes are regarded not in a sense of subjective phenomena—rather, they are objective macrocosmic and microcosmic principles that belong to the sphere of *anima mundi*. The staff, as a symbol of a spine, a cosmic tree, or resurrection, was adopted by the Hellenes from ancient Mesopotamia. Hermes' role as a messenger can have a twofold interpretation—an earthly one and an angelic one, as he is the bringer and harbinger of sacred truths.

Hermes is also regarded as the ancestor of the family that oversaw the Eleusinian Mysteries. Autolycus, the grandfather of Odysseus, known for his cunning and trickery, is said to be the real son of Hermes (*Od.* XIX.396). Each stolen good and each unexpected finding are thought to be a gift from Hermes (*hermaion*). As the ruler of borders, Hermes assists in communication between different levels of being, as well as different cultures. An interpreter of mysteries, an exegete of symbols, a commentator of literary texts and a translator—all of this is a *hermēneus*, whose patron is Hermes. A hermeneut takes the realities of a certain ontological level and translates them into the discourse of another level; he explains the components of one culture through the terms of another culture.

In a way, Hermes can be regarded as *logos*, the language of gods and men that follows a set of preliminary rules. Interpretation liberates one from darkness and leads into logical clarity, just as Osiris' soul (*ba*) travels into the sacred light (*akh*) in Egyptian mysteries. This hermeneutic aspect of the Hellenic god, related to the possibility of symbolic interpretation and the revelation of truth, is comparable to the functions of Thoth. However, some qualities of the Greek Hermes do not have anything in common with the qualities of Thoth, the scribe of gods. As a deity of merchants, carrying a bag of money in his right hand, the Roman Mercury deviates from his Greek and Egyptian counterparts, even though the perpetual dialectics of trade, trickery and theft closely connects him with the image of the cattle-stealing Hermes.

Sometimes, the depiction of Hermes is merged with Aphrodite, thus creating Hermaphroditus. Even though vulgarized by fiction, Hermaphroditus is actually a cosmogonic character; he is a primordial deity, split into two halves, two cosmic principles, like the Etruscan *turms* and *turan*, Greek *ho turannos* (a male ruler) and *hē turannos* (a female ruler). The dialectics of the relationship of this couple is determined by Love. In the Orphic cosmogonies, the hermaphroditic deity that emerges from the Cosmic Egg (like the Egyptian Atum, who ascends from the depths of Nun) is called Phanes. In some aspects, Hermes represents the Primordial Baby, a winged child, carried on the back of a dolphin. It is thought that hermas, the sculptures that mark borders and ward off evil spirits, were initially built on mountains, which symbolize the primeval hill, underneath which, in a cave, baby Hermes is born. The birth of this child represents the rhythmical-musical dispersion of cosmic rays, as the tortoise (whose shell was used for making the lyre) and a dolphin are the iconographic hypostases of Apollo.

· THOTH, THE SCRIBE OF THE GODS ·

In the *Pyramid Texts*, which are the oldest known corpus of religious works, Thoth (*dhwty*) governs the night sky, while Horus—the daytime sky. That is why the deceased call upon Thoth, the god of the West, who appears in the form of the setting sun (which is represented by a symbolic mask) and who is comparable to Atum, the embodiment of Being itself. As the theurgical ascent of a deceased ruler of Egypt (who embodies humanity, as well as the spiritual reality) marks the archetypal axis of the reintegration of being, Thoth oversees this ascent as the guide and patron of regal souls.

Egyptian texts mention that Thoth came into existence when the seed of Horus entered the body of Set. The birth of Thoth from the forehead of Horus' rival Set is akin to the birth of Athena, who is born from the head of Zeus. According to another version of the myth, a golden disc emerges from Set's forehead, which Thoth catches and places on his own head. However, the origins of Thoth are rarely discussed, if at all, though the Egyptian *Book of the Dead* mentions that he was "[the] son of Aner, coming forth from the two Aners" (CXXXIV.L6). Unfortunately, E. A. Wallis Budge, the translator of the work, never explained the meaning of this phrase.[3] Maybe Aner here is actually Aker, the lion-shaped deity that guards the gates of the horizon, often represented as a pair of lions or sphinxes with the Sun rising in-between them.

Together with his wife Maat, the goddess of cosmic order and the personification of truth, Thoth stands on the barge of the Sun god, as if he is leading the way. However, the expression "the Sun god" is not very accurate, as the visible disc of the Sun is merely a symbol of the invisible Ra. Nevertheless, it is difficult to avoid this connotation, established by the bi-

---

3. E. A. Wallis Budge, *From Fetish to God in Ancient Egypt*, Dover Publications, New York, 1988, p. 157.

ased Christian and modernistic hermeneutics that managed to reduce all the Egyptian gods to their corresponding natural phenomena.

Ra, Maat and Thoth arise from the primeval depths of Nun. This ascension symbolises the emergence of the sacred Intellect from the depths of the inexpressible One, talking in Neoplatonic terminology. The dispersion of the noetic light, which is equivalent to the dispersion of sound, represents the manifestation of being by establishing the levels of the noetic cosmos, or the sphere of spiritual lights.

Thoth is also referred to as the heart and tongue of Ra, i.e. the demiurgic Intellect and the world-creating Word. It means that Thoth disperses and organizes archetypes, or Platonic Ideas, which appear in the form of articulated hieroglyphs. These are called *medu neter* (words of nature or divine speech). They encompass the whole spectre of theophanies. Researchers accurately compare this wisdom to the theory of Plato's Ideas as well as the concept of *logos*, cultivated by Middle Platonists.

As he pronounces the demiurgic words or writes in hieroglyphs, Thoth embodies the noetic will of Ra. He transforms the cause into the effect, thus creating or, more accurately, unfolding the world, bringing the unknown into the light. Thoth's speech creates Heaven and Earth. Thus, a noetic paradigm becomes a psychical and physical phenomenon. That is why it is evident that Thoth's speech can resurrect from the dead. Instructed by Thoth, Isis magically revives Osiris and conceives Horus, who also receives help from Thoth's words when he is stung by the scorpion that represents the power of Set.

According to E. A. Wallis, the temple texts of the Late Period of Egypt confirm that "Thoth was regarded as a god who was self-begotten and self-produced, that he was the One, that he made the calculations concerning the stablishing of the heavens, and the stars, and the earth, that he was the heart of Ra, that he was the master of law both in its physical and moral conceptions, and that he had the knowledge of 'divine speech.'"[4] The heart of Ra (which is the ultimate manifestation of all the intellectual potencies of light) appears in the form of Thoth, who is the "twice-great" or "thrice-great" ruler of sacred words, the lord of Truth (Maat). Some researchers attempt to translate these epithets into the language of mathematics. As E. A. Wallis puts it, "in Ptolemaic and later times Thoth was called 'Great Great' which the Rosetta Stone, 1.19, rendered by Megas Kai Megas. [...] The name of Thoth followed by the sign for 'great' repeated eight times has been found in a Demotic papyrus".[5] Here, the first phrase can be expressed by $2a$, while the latter—by a formula $(2a)^3$. Thus, *trismegistos* means "twice-great cubed". However, it is difficult to say whether these speculations are credible. Nevertheless, Thoth actually rules over the eight archetypal principles, which transcend the noetic cosmos and represent the Ogdoad—the eight primordial deities worshipped in Hermopolis whose name, in turn, can be translated as "Eight-Town".

Throughout the years, the role of the Demiurge was given to different Egyptian gods. In the Late Period, the demiurgic aspect of Thoth is not really explored upon, emphasizing the myth of the articulation of sacred words (*medu neter*), or hieroglyphs, rather than the myth of the emergence from the watery depths of Nun. Widely speaking, Thoth is the founder and patron of Egyptian literature, the lord of all the books that follow the example of the archetypal Book (the entirety of noetic hieroglyphs). Thoth rules over all the manifestations of both celestial and earthly wisdom. It is not a mere coincidence that the Islamic civilization compares the sacred Intellect (the Neoplatonic *Nous*) to a pen, *qalam*. In this regard, Thoth is a self-writing Word or the Script that moulds the architectonic of being.

In Egyptian mythology, the miracle of the manifestation of being (*kheper*) is personified by Heka, the god of cosmologi-

---

4. E. A. Wallis Budge, *The Gods of the Egyptians. Studies in Egyptian Mythology*, vol. I, Dover Publications, New York, 1969, p. 401.
5. E. A. Wallis Budge, *From Fetish to God in Ancient Egypt*, p. 157.

cal magic who sometimes transcends even the solar Intellect. Heka can be compared to the world-creating Maya from Hindu philosophy. It is the Word that governs the manifestations and transformations of being; and it leads one down the path of demiurgic descent and theurgical ascent. That is why *heka* is the word of liturgical power, which can be comprehended as a transformative word of God, analogous to a Hindu mantra. The words of power (*hekau*) create the world; they also help to ascend to the primordial streams, thus reversing the sequence of ontological (and, in a way, semiotical) metamorphoses. Thoth is the master of these words of power and the arch-mage of all possible transformations, imitated by sorcerers and servants of his cult.

Thoth's verdict is final and definitive, for he is the primordial Judge who makes peace between humans and gods, and who maintains universal justice in both worlds—on Earth and in the realm of the dead (the Egyptian Duat). He is also the judge of the archetypal pair of the gods that symbolize the duality of this world. The Pharaoh embodies both Horus and Set, thus representing the integrity of light and darkness, the wholeness of the sacred image (*tut*). That is why Thoth, "Judge of the Rehehui, the pacifier of the gods, who dwelleth in Unnu (Hermopolis), the great god in the Temple of Abtiti",[6] restores the order and balance of the universe. Thoth plays an important role in the battle between Ra and Apep, as well as the battle between Horus Behdety and Set, which represent the same archetypal model. He cleanses and restores the Eye of the Sun (Ra), gouged out by Set, and gives Isis a head of a cow when she is beheaded by Horus, who is enraged when his mother does not allow him to annihilate Set, the murderer of his father Osiris. The rejuvenation of the eye is an especially important motif, as it symbolizes unity and the restoration of primordial spir-

---

6. E. A. Wallis Budge, *The Gods of the Egyptians. Studies in Egyptian Mythology*, vol. I, p. 405.

itual existence, together with physical, psychical and intellectual integrity. That is why every offering, no matter what it consisted of, was referred to as the Eye of Horus in ancient Egypt. Each offering represented the restoration of unity and integrity: a deity is presented with a unified archetypal image, i.e. the intact Eye.

Thoth finds it important to maintain the balance of the cosmos and the periodical shift between light and darkness. That is the reason why he does not permit the victory of either Horus or Set, which would result in the destruction of one or the other. This preserves the liturgical and theurgical flow of the Year and introduces the mythical calendar, which is based on the cosmological drama of the gods. Here, Thoth manifests as an astronomer, mathematician and measurer; however, he presents himself not as an earthly sage, but rather as a god who determines the cycle of seasons and the movement of the celestial bodies. In this way, he is the first Pythagorean (if such an analogy can be made), the one who sets the proportions, dimensions, movement and duration of the Pythagorean cosmos. That is why all the other gods know their place and thus can be proper followers of Ra whose purpose, function, trajectories and ranks are determined by Thoth's decisions, which express the will of the highest Intellect. The transformation of souls (*bau*) in Duat, i.e. their journey toward noetic light, also depends on Thoth's eternal wisdom—the knowledge of the words that weave the content of the universe or, more accurately, the ontic-semiotic confirmation of the Ideas that determine the true spiritual identity.

As an archetypal author and a wisdom authority, Thoth is attributed with various texts, or "chapters", that comprise different versions of the Egyptian *Book of the Dead*. Some of them are claimed to be written by his own hand. Thoth also supposedly wrote the *Book of Breathing* that teaches souls how to breathe eternally in order to continue living and become gods, just like the souls of the gods that form the heart of Ra, and that they could belong to the great God (*Pert em hru* CXCVII). In the Netherworld, Thoth protects Osiris (as well as the deceased, who are equivalent to Osiris) by granting him dark powers and the words that overcome mental obstacles and restore the ideal model of being together with the sacred primordial identity. In this play of initiation and posthumous alchemical transformations, Thoth is a mystagogue and the lord of transformative power: through him, Osiris becomes Ra, and the winged *ba* merges with the noetic light *akh*.

That is why Thoth is also the judge of the dead. He stands before the scales in the Hall of Two Truths, ready to announce the verdict after weighing the heart of the deceased. On one side of the scales lies the heart (the symbol of intellect and conscience), while the other side displays a feather that symbolizes truth (*maat*). Sometimes scriptures indicate that Thoth weighs words instead of actions, i.e. he matches the soul with its spiritual paradigm. A vindicated soul becomes *maakheru*—the one who speaks truth. In turn, his words are *maa*, i.e. they have the demiurgical power to transform an idea into an object, as well as to actualize semiotic realia into the spiritual realm and recognize them as paradigms. The one who has been blessed as *maakheru* speaks in the words that have the power to create reality. Everything that has been said materializes, and that is why the precision of speech and the pronunciation of demiurgical intonations are so important. In a way, it is a reiteration of ritualistic cosmogony that leads toward one's true identity, or the union with the highest Principle.

Liturgical rites and prayers are also based on the "light-bringing" power of words. This power renews the connection between the archetype and the image. Only Thoth, the god of wisdom, can teach these magical words because he is the founder of religious rites, the builder of primordial temples and the architect of being. His hieroglyphs position objects into their proper place and set their boundaries. The knowledge of the secret names transforms the demons of the Duat (which can be seen as path-blocking karmic complexes or the consequences of false identities) into helpers and integrates them into the consciousness of the soul. As the fabric of cosmic manifestations is woven by the power of the Word, the path to primordial principles can be seen as a movement through text. Death and spiritual rebirth in Duat are metaphysical Hermeneutic processes that lead into the perennial vault of sacred light—firstly, into Osiris' Field of Reeds, or the Field of Offerings, then—into the Boat of Millions of Years and, finally, into the depths of the unknown.

According to E. A. Wallis Budge, one of Thoth's temples in Hermopolis was called Het Abtit, or "the House of the Net", where a sacred net was preserved and venerated.[7] In Egyptian mythology, a net is not only a tool—it is also a symbol of the fabric of the universe. The processes of tying and untying a knot symbolize imprisonment and liberation. One myth mentions a net, stretched out between Heaven and Earth, used by baboons (iconographic symbols of Thoth) to capture the souls of the dead. In order to avoid this net, one needs to audibly pronounce its components. Only then the obstacle is bypassed and integrated into the semantic horizon of the deceased, who becomes a fisherman, i.e. a bearer of sacred wisdom. Similarly to this myth, Plotinus compares the material universe to a net: "The universe lies in soul which bears it up, and nothing is without a share of soul. It is as if a net immersed in the waters were alive, but unable to make its own that in which it is. The sea is already spread out and the net spreads with it, as far as it can; for no one of its parts can be anywhere else than where it lies" (*Enn.* IV.3.9).

Thoth belongs to various theological triads like Ptah-Horus-Thoth, Ra-Horus-Thoth and Osiris-Horus-Thoth. Sometimes Thoth is referred to as the heart of Ptah or the throat of He Who Hides His Name (*Amen-ren-f*), from which comes the demiurgic Word. A few of his other titles are the Ox of the Sky, the White Disc, the Messenger of Ra and the Ruler of Stars.

---

7. *Ibid.*, p. 405.

· THE TRADITIONAL ICONOGRAPHY OF THOTH ·

E. A. Wallis writes that "the name of the god Thoth, Tehuti, appears to be derived from the supposed oldest name of the ibis in Egypt, i.e., *tehu*, to which the termination *ti* has been added, with the idea of indicating that the king called Tehuti possessed the qualities and attributes of the ibis. A derivation of the name which appears to have been favoured by the Egyptians connected it with the word *tekh*, 'a weight'".[8] The latter is visually depicted as a heart. According to Horapollo, an author of Late Antiquity, the Egyptians use the symbol of ibis for writing the word "heart" because this bird belongs to Hermes—"master of the heart and reason in all men" (*Hierogl.* I.36).

The Egyptian word for the sacred ibis (*threskiornis aethiopicus*) was *hab*, or *heb*. During the Late and Ptolemaic periods, the ibis was especially revered. Numerous mummified birds were found at burial sites. Statues of the ibis, made from alabaster, wood and gold, were also discovered. The head, legs and tail of the bird are made of darker materials. The contrast between black and white symbolizes the difference between the inner psyche and outward expression. The sculptures of ibis are often paired with the sculptures of goddess Maat. This sacred bird is also associated with Ptah, Osiris, Imhotep, Hathor and Nephthys. The drawing of an ibis (in this case—*geronticus eremita*) is a determinative of the word *akh*, which means spiritual glory, noetic light and the transfigured soul that belongs to the domain of the solar Intellect.

As the scribe of the gods, Thoth is usually depicted as having the body of a human and the head of an ibis. He holds a sceptre and the hieroglyph *ankh*, which symbolizes life. Different aspects of Thoth are represented by different headwear. The crescent moon and the lunar disc on Thoth's head represent him as the ruler of time and the calendar. When

---

8. *Ibid.*, pp. 405–406.

Thoth holds a writing palette and a reed, he is depicted as the scribe of Maat. When Thoth is associated with Ra's emergence from the depths of Nun, he holds the symbol of *udjat*— the Eye of Ra. Thoth can also manifest as Aah Tehuti, the god of the Moon:

> The great god, the lord of heaven, the king of the gods, the maker of eternity and creator of everlastingness. Under this form the god Thoth is depicted: 1. As a mummy, standing upon the symbol of *maat*, and holding in his hands the emblems of "life", "stability", "sovereignty and dominion", and the sceptre; on his head is the crescent moon, and by the side of his head he has the lock of hair, symbolic of youth. 2. As a bearded, mummied human figure with the crescent moon on his head, and the lock of hair symbolic of youth. The head, however, has two faces, which are intended, presumably, to represent the periods of the waxing and the waning of the moon.[9]

The Eye of Thoth, or *utchat*, is the left eye of Ra. It represents the winter half of the year, while the right eye of Ra represents the summer half of the year. These doctrines are similar to the cosmological teachings of Hindu Upanishads. E. A. Wallis writes: "This *Utchat* of Thoth, or of Thoth-Horus, as it should more correctly be called, is mentioned in the *Pyramid Texts*, where it is called the 'Black Eye of Horus'; thus of King Unas it is said, 'Thou hast seized the two Eyes of Horus, the White Eye and the Black Eye, and thou hast carried them off and set them in front of thee and they give light to thy face.' The White Eye here referred to is, of course, the sun."[10] The eye of Thoth-Horus is depicted in accordance with certain proportions that mathematically express cosmological truths and illustrate the artistic principles of geometry. From

---

9. *Ibid.*, pp. 402.
10. *Ibid.*, pp. 427.

the perspective of the reader, the eye of the Sun points to the left, while the eye of the Moon points to the right.

According to various myths, Thoth heals both of these eyes and restores their integrity. In a metaphysical sense, it is the revival of sacred unity, the return to the balance and integrity of the archetype, the restoration of the Golden Age in a mythical, liturgical, ritualistic, philosophical and alchemical sense. The metaphysics of the Eye of God becomes the paradigm of the manifestation of Being and the basis for the entire cult.

Thoth can also be depicted as a baboon (*ian, aan*). These words are related to the verb "to write" (*an*). It is thought that, during the archaic period of Egypt, there was a deity called Baba, whose name carried on to *papio hamadryas*. Baboons are also referred to as "the eastern souls" (*bau*) that greet the rising Sun, which is an epiphany of the sacred Intellect, representing a cosmogonic act—the creation of all the levels of being and the manifestation of the world. In a way, they are equivalent to the angels of later theologies. On the contrary, "western souls" (*bau*) are the jackals of Anubis. However, in the mentioned context of solar metaphysics, it is not accurate to translate *bau* as "souls", as this word represents celestial beings, manifestations of primordial principles and symbolic epiphanies of gods.

In Egyptian mythology, the baboon has many depictions which demonstrate the importance of this animal. For example, it is sometimes portrayed sitting on a shoulder or a head of a scribe, as if guiding his thoughts toward the right direction. Similarly, Thoth's baboon sits on top of the scales in the Hall of Two Truths, where the hearts of the dead are weighted. The gates of Duat are also guarded by a baboon. Four baboons sit at the four corners of the Lake of Fire—an alchemical furnace, whose flames are torture for the wicked but do not harm the blessed. Sometimes the baboon is depicted holding the eye of *utchat* or sitting on the barge of Ra that sails through the sky. In this regard, it is both a lunar and a solar being, thus expressing the complex nature of Thoth.

· COSMOGONIC RITUALS AND SYMBOLS ·

According to E. A. Wallis, "the oldest seat of the cult of Thoth was Unu-Resu, 'Unu of the South', the capital of the Hare nome, i.e. the XVth nome of Upper Egypt; the Greeks called it Hermopolis. There Thoth was regarded as the head of an Ogdoad, or company of eight primeval gods, four gods who were frog-headed, and four goddesses who were serpent-headed."[11] Together with Thoth, this Ogdoad becomes an Ennead, which exist in the depths of Nun before the manifestation of being and the emergence of the noetic cosmos.

When discussing the theology of Thoth, researchers often compare it with the prologue of the Gospel of John, recognizing the Christian concept of *Logos* not only in Middle Platonism, but also in ancient Egyptian cosmogony. However, we should not depict the theological schools of Hermopolis, Memphis or Heliopolis as rivalling institutions. It seems that such separation of "local cults" is only partly correct. Nowadays, researchers prefer the notion of multifaceted unity, which carries a myriad of symbolic perspectives, thus creating new "iconic" structures of theological worldview that fit various liturgical paradigms.

The role of the Demiurge of the universe can be played by various gods (or different manifestations of the same Primordial Principle). Ptah, the patron of Memphis, can also represent the Supreme Principle and the "technical Demiurge" (*technikos nous*), as noted by Proclus, who compared Ptah to the Greek Hephaestus (*In Tim.* I.147.8). Guided by Thoth and Maat, Ptah creates the world according to Thoth's archetypal plan. Khnum, who is also referred to as "Divine Potter", spins his pottery wheel and moulds the first human together with the human's *ka*—the vital principle. Khnum is depicted as a man with the head of a ram, often sitting at a pottery wheel, creating human life out of clay, while Thoth stands nearby,

---

11. E. A. Wallis Budge, *The Gods of the Egyptians. Studies in Egyptian Mythology*, vol. I, p. 427.

holding a palm branch, slit as many times as the human has years to live. This implies that Thoth is the Divine Providence that governs fate and the world of paradigms, and acts in the name of truth, justice and cosmic harmony.

The Egyptian god Un, who is depicted as a hare, is similar to Thoth. The feminine side of Un is the goddess Unut. According to a legend, the son of Khufu found a chapter of the *Book of the Dead,* written down by Thoth himself. The chapter was later marked as CXXXVII. The goddess Unut is depicted as a woman with the head of a hare, holding knives in her hands. However, she actually has two different forms. One of them belongs to the southern Hermopolis (Unu, Khemennu), another—to the northern Hermopolis (Unnu, Meht, Hermopolis Parva), where Thoth is worshipped in the form of Ap-rehui together with his feminine aspect—Nehemauait.

Just like the goddess Maat, Unut, the ruler of Hermopolis, is closely related to Thoth, who, in this case, can be compared to the hare-headed Un. In the temple of Dendera, the latter is depicted as a mummy. In this aspect, he is equivalent to Osiris, the ruler of the afterlife, especially when keeping in mind that one of the epithets of Osiris, *Un-nefer,* can be read as "the beautiful Un". Just like a hare, Osiris "leaps into" the Netherworld and gets resurrected, similarly to how the Sun "leaps out" of the world of darkness, or the womb of Nut, the cow goddess. As we can see, the qualities of different gods and goddesses intertwine, creating a noetic fabric that resembles the structure of a labyrinth.

The writings on the Shabaka Stone, which include *the Memphite Theology,* reflect the concepts of the Old Kingdom about the creation of the world by Thought and Word. In these writings, Thoth is referred to as the tongue of Ptah, who, in turn, creates every single object and hieroglyph in the universe. Here, hieroglyphs (*medu neter*) refer to the noetic Forms, or Platonic Ideas, that comprise all the components of the reality and that are expressed by the visible archetypes of being. Thoth is the ruler of all these hieroglyphs, and he articulates the reality in accordance with eternal noetic examples.

Speaking in the metaphorical terms of Egyptian metaphysics, his heart translates his thoughts into an articulated and written language. This translation symbolizes a cosmogonic process. A written symbol (or an eidetic drawing), an object and its name all appear together; however, from the perspective of the material object, the hieroglyph plays the role of the Form (*eidos*). The entirety of hieroglyphs is akin to the sacred Book of Thoth—a prototype of the Qur'an that encompasses all the archetypes of being.

The mentioned text (which did not survive in its entirety because the Shabaka Stone had been used as a millstone) mentions the ogdoad of the primordial gods who existed before the manifestation of being. Similar ogdoads, whose elements (i.e. the names of principles) vary, exist in the theological systems of Hermopolis and Thebes. The names of the deities that comprise the primordial ogdoad are transliterated inconsistently and thus are difficult to translate. Speaking in Neoplatonic terms, this ogdoad dwelled in the depths of the inexpressible One before the light of the sacred Intellect was manifested, i.e. before the creation of the noetic, psychical and physical being. To emphasize the apophatic nature of these transcendental principles, they are depicted as humans with the heads of serpents and frogs. These are Nun and Naunet (water), Heh and Hauhet (infinity), Kek and Kauket (darkness), and Amun and Amunet (invisibility).

Sometimes, four masculine principles, led by Thoth, are distinguished from the ogdoad of Hermopolis. In the Middle Kingdom and later, the high priest of Hermopolis was referred to as "the greatest out of five". This might have represented Thoth. One papyrus contains a prayer to "the five great gods of Hermopolis" (*Le papyrus magique Harris* III.5). This same papyrus contains a spell against crocodiles, which needs to be uttered in front of a clay icon of Amon, who stands on a crocodile and is depicted as a human with four heads of a ram. He is greeted by a group of baboons who represent the Ogdoad of Hermopolis (*ibid*. VI.9). In the level of the lower world, the timeless cosmogonic process is symbolized, repeated and embodied by the floods of the Nile, when snakes and frogs emerge ("are born") from the mud. They are visible symbolic images of the primordial Ogdoad of the gods.

According to L. Lamy, it is not accurate to refer to Nun as the primordial chaos in the biblical sense, because she rather represents an undefined, eternal and never-ending sub-stance—the source of the Universe.[12] The term of "chaos", as it is understood today, means a disorder of material things or their components. It does not have anything in common with the concepts of the noetic cosmos or the apophatic "depth" that transcends it. This depth is the Neoplatonic One, referred to as God by Proclus. The relationship between the absolute transcendence (from the perspective of the sacred Intellect) and the noetic cosmos (which is the synthesis of both psychi-cal and physical reality, united by the Demiurge) is symbol-ized by a lotus flower, emerging from water and mud, which also represents the four archetypal elements. From this flower emerges the noetic Sun—the god Atum-Ra, whose presence enlightens the world of all the psychical and physical levels of being—the macrocosmic and microcosmic reality.

That is why the members of the Ogdoad, who dwell in the depths of Nun, are referred to as the fathers and mothers of Ra. Ra emerges from the lotus flower, whose stem grows from an invisible octagonal mandala. One cannot compare Ra to the visible Sun disc, as Ra creates the archetypal world of Ideas. He is the invisible reason behind the visible light, and the light that engulfs the material cosmos is merely a reflec-tion of the noetic cosmos, which is considered as ontologi-cally higher.

Similarly, the Shabaka Stone identifies the god Ptah not only with Nun and Naunet (whom E. Iversen compares with the "higher" and "lower" waters that are mentioned in the Bible: Gen. I.7)[13] but also with Tatenen—the primordial

---

12. Lucie Lamy, *Egyptian Mysteries. New Light on Ancient Knowledge*, Thames and Hudson, London, 1991, p. 10.

13. Erik Iversen, *Egyptian and Hermetic Doctrine*, Museum Tusculanum Press, Copenhagen, 1984, p. 8.

mound, and Nefertem, who emerges from a lotus flower and who represents the solar Intellect and its perennial beauty. The theological tradition of Memphis speaks of Nun, the father of the gods, who becomes a member of the ogdoad. The emergence of Ptah (the manifestation into being, *kheper*) means the materialization of the world. Ptah, who dwells in the primeval depths, becomes the father and mother of Atum, as Atum symbolizes the noetic integrity.

In the form of a manifested deity, Ptah is "everything". The universe appears by his command, just like hieroglyphs (*medu neter*)—the words that embody the will of God the creator. The physically perceived universe is the physical body of Ptah. It is not a mere coincidence that the symbolic cipher, used in the Late Period, depicts his name as the hieroglyphs that represent the Sky, the Earth and the infinity.

The visible universe (in the words of Plutarch, *kosmos aisthetos*) can be compared to Horus the Younger, while the state of non-being—which existed before the demiurgical Word and the creation of the universe—can be compared to Horus the Great (*De Iside et Osiride* 54.373c). The heart and tongue of Ptah (*Nous and Logos*) manifest, or come into being (*kheper*), in the form of Atum. The same role can be played by Thoth. The power of the sacred heart and tongue permeates his body, the mouths and the bodies of all the other gods, as well as all the humans and animals. Foremost of Powers (*sekhem*) is one of the epithets of Ptah. This power manifests as a noetic intention of the heart (or a demiurgic thought) and the language that embodies the thought. The power of the heart and the tongue (i.e. intellect and logical discourse) of all living beings is the reflection of the sacred principle.

Such a universe is open to sacred interpretation, revealed and maintained by Thoth, the god of wisdom. A homologous bond is established between celestial and earthly events, between sacred archetypes and images, and between cosmogonic examples and ritualistic-liturgical actions that echo the events that happened during the First Time (*tep zepi*), which is a timeless present. Thoth, or a hermeneut that impersonates him, reveals the anagogical meaning behind cosmic processes and manifestations. The art of hermeneutics shows the way of descendance and ascension. Moving in a circle, it marks the mythical horizon of being, which can be perceived as a sanctum that reveals the hierarchy of sacred manifestations. This universe, created and maintained by heliophanies (the rays of the solar Intellect), is worshipped and interpreted as the entirety of mythical creatures, names and hieroglyphs. It cannot be explained from the perspective of natural science. The term "nature", as it is understood today, did not exist in ancient Egypt, because then, reality was regarded as a multifaceted body of the gods (*neteru*), a kind of cult statue, revived by the noetic life (*ankh*). That is why the matter of reality consists of iconographic signs and symbols.

Interpretation is regarded as a ritual, while the ritual itself is a liturgical and semiotic portrayal of cosmogony. The performance of sacred rites (with the right knowledge of their semantics) maintains the order of the world (*maat*), which consists of external and internal aspects of celestial actions. The manifested being is identical to the ritual performed by gods, which is, in a way, echoed by the rites performed in temples. In this entirety of theurgical relations, knowledge (*gnosis*) and action (*praxis*) are inseparable.

The Universe can be regarded as a metaphysical Book. Here, every part has a certain symbolic load and mythical meaning. As spiritual phenomena are usually conveyed as metaphors, it appears that the intellectual and physical realities nearly merge. However, sacred primordial principles are always prioritized. To "know" means to understand the mythical structures, paradigms, hieroglyphs (Platonic Ideas), sacred iconography and its metaphysical meaning, the names of the gods and the typical situations of demiurgic semiotics. "He who knows this is made in the image of the Great God"— states a text from the period of the New Kingdom. This is the perennial doctrine of *imago dei*, revealed to us by the sacred knowledge of Thoth.

· MAAT AND OTHER GODDESSES ASSOCIATED WITH THOTH ·

Maat, one of the most important concepts of ancient Egypt, means truth, justice, order, balance and harmony. Goddess Maat is depicted as a sitting woman, usually winged, with an ostrich feather on her head. She is the daughter of Ra and the wife of Thoth. Together with Thoth, she stands on the solar barge, which emerges from the primordial waters (Nun). This emphasizes the harmony of the noetic cosmos, mirrored by the material cosmos. In the latter, the pharaoh, who is referred to as the son of Ra, periodically restores disrupted order and justice. One hymn, which is dedicated to Ra, states that everyday, Thoth and Maat determine the way of the solar barge, steered by Horus. Amun-Ra rests in Truth (Maat) and lives by it. Maat is also called the Eye of Ra, the ruler of Heaven, Earth and Duat.

In her double form of Maati, or the goddess of the Upper and Lower Egypt, she represents justice in Duat. The feather used for weighing the souls of the dead at the Hall of Two Truths actually belongs to Maat. During the trial, the deceased tries to convince Osiris of being pure and truthful. As the word of Thoth created the universe, it is Thoth who has the right to pronounce the name of the vindicated soul so that it would acquire a spiritual body of light and be reborn in the kingdom of Osiris. In a way, Thoth and Maat perform the "philosophical" function, if philosophy is regarded in a Pythagorean and Platonic sense as a preparation for death, the purification of soul (for it to be worthy of truth) and the connection with sacred principles. Phonetically, *maat* can refer to many concepts. E. A. Wallis Budge writes:

> The hieroglyphic, which also has the phonetic value of Maat, is described by some as a "cubit", i.e., the measure of a cubit, and by others as a "flute", which would, presumably, be made of reed. [...] About the meaning of the word *maat*, there is, fortunately, no difficulty, for from many passages in texts of

all periods we learn that it is indicated primarily "that which is straight," and it was probably the name which was given to the instrument by which the work of the handicraftsman of every kind was kept straight; as far as we can see the same ideas which were attached to the Greek word *kanon* (which first of all seems to have meant any *straight rod* used to keep things straight, then a *rule* used by masons, and finally, metaphorically, a rule, or law, or canon, by which the lives of men and their actions were kept straight and governed) belong to the Egyptian word *maat*. The Egyptians used the word in a physical and moral sense, and thus it came to mean "right, true, truth, real, genuine, upright, righteous, just, steadfast, unalterable," etc.; *khesbet maat* is "real lapis-lazuli" as opposed to blue paste; *shes maat* means "ceaselessly and regularly," *em un maat* indicates that a thing is really so, the man who is good, and honest is *maat*, the truth (*maat*) is great and mighty, and "it hath never been broken since the time of Osiris"; finally, the exact equivalent of the English words "God will judge the right" is found in the Egyptian *pa neter apu pa maat*.[14]

Seshat, the goddess of architecture, knowledge and writing, is also closely identified with Thoth, who can be depicted as her father or husband. She governs the fields of wisdom and hieroglyphs. Her symbol is a seven-petal flower on a stem, or a star, surrounded by a symmetrical pair of horns turned upside down. Seshat is depicted as a woman dressed in a leopard hide, wearing the mentioned symbol on top of her head. She is "the Mistress of the House of Books", the patron of libraries and literature. Sometimes in her right hand Seshat holds a pen, while in the other—an oval cartouche. As a helper of Thoth, she is an expert and scribe of names, in charge of the semiotic text of the universe and who informs Osiris of the names of the righteous. Seshat can also hold a palm branch, which she uses to track the passage of time by

---

14. E. A. Wallis Budge, *The Gods of the Egyptians. Studies in Egyptian Mythology*, vol. I, p. 417.

inscribing small notches. The palm branch itself stands on a frog that sits on *shen*, a symbol that represents infinity. On the top of the palm rests the emblem of Sed festivals. In this aspect, Seshat manages the royal calendar, giving the pharaoh a lifespan equivalent to the "years of Ra", as if including his name into the register of the eternal Ideas.

On a cosmogonic level, Seshat is the assistant of Thoth-demiurge, while in the earthly realm she is responsible for all the matters regarding architecture, construction, history and chronology. With her own hands, she writes down all the accomplishments of the ruler—the son of Ra, whose tomb is built according to her plan. In various aspects, this goddess is identified with Isis, who is referred to as the sister of Osiris, the mother of the golden Horus and the daughter of Nut. Sometimes Seshat is merged with Nehemauait, another goddess of Thoth's constellation, who is the daughter of Ra and the "holy ruler of Khemenu (Hermopolis)". In a way, she is a hypostasis of the goddess Hathor, who is depicted with a headdress of cow horns and a sun disk on her head. In the right hand she holds a papyrus staff, while in the other— a statue of Maat. Her face is also traditionally depicted on the sistrum, a musical instrument used for various rituals. It wards off negative energies and the evil spirits of Set. That is why Egyptian priestesses and noblewomen are portrayed with a sistrum in their hands. It is the instrument of Hathor. Nehemauait can manifest herself as Mehurt, the cow goddess who gave birth to the sun. Mehurt is a hypostasis of Hathor, Isis, Nut and Neith; this hypostasis represents the power of integrity and is equivalent to the Eye of Ra, which is a universal symbol of creative power that speaks about cosmogonic processes and the course of internal transformation, birth and alchemical rebirth.

The multifaceted associations of Hathor are reflected by her varying iconography. She can be portrayed not only as a celestial cow, but also as a pregnant woman with engorged breasts, or a woman with the head of a cow smelling a lotus flower, which appears as one of the symbols that represent Upper and Lower Egypt. It might be the primordial lotus, from which the very first solar deity emerged at the beginning of time. Some sources state that Hathor, as the perpetual ruler of the city of the Ogdoad, helped Thoth create the first objects of the ethereal world. During the Early Dynastic Period of Egypt, the hall of Maati, where Thoth weighs the value of words, was referred to as the hall of the cow Mehurt. From this point of view, the judgement of the dead is held in the belly of the celestial cow.

· THE DIVINE IMHOTEP ·

Together with Hermes Trismegistus (whose anthropomorphized image is modelled after Thoth), Asclepius is among the most important characters of Hermetic literature. However, his paradigm is not only mythical-theological, but also historical. In the Greek mythological tradition, Asclepius is referred to as the son of Apollo the Helper, Doctor and the Muse-Leader (Epikourios, Iatros, Mousagetes). Worshipped in the temple of Epidaurus, Asclepius healed pilgrims through sacred sleep (incubation) and was able to manifest himself as a snake. One of the letters, supposedly written by Hippocrates, states that Hippocrates witnessed a manifestation of Asclepius: "Serpents followed him, enormous sort of reptiles, they too hurrying on, with their tremendous train of coils, making a whistling noise as in the wilderness and woodland glens. His associates followed him carrying boxes of drugs, tightly bound. Then the god stretched forth his hand to me. And taking it gladly I begged him to join me and not to be too late to aid me in my treatment."[15]

Aelius Aristides, the author of *Sacred Tales* who experienced the epiphanies of Serapis, Isis and Asclepius, describes the manifestation of Asclepius as an ecstatic mystical experience. The consciousness of Aristides was transformed and

---

15. *Asclepius. A Collection and Interpretation of the Testimonies I*, ed. E. J. L. and L. Edelstein, Baltimore, 1945, p. 259.

he was granted the name of Theodorus, thus becoming akin to a god. During the last episode of his mystical vision of Asclepius, he was allowed to witness "what Plato referred to as the Soul of the World."[16]

In the tradition of Hellenic Egypt, Asclepius was identified with Imhotep, who was often referred to as "the second Asclepius". He is a deified sage, priest and architect of the Old Kingdom who became the hypostasis of the theology of Ptah, the patron of Memphis.

As a demiurge of the cosmos and the patron of craftsmanship, Ptah could manifest himself in various forms, for example, 1) Ptah-Nun (a primordial principle), 2) Ptah-Hapis (transcendent Nile), 3) Ptah-Tanen (the primordial mound), and 4) Ptah-Aten (the glowing disc of the Sun). The goddess Sekhmet (the wife of Ptah) and their son Nefertum formed the triad of Memphis. However, Nefertum was eventually replaced by Imhotep.

Sekhmet is the divine potential (Gk. *dunamis*) or the celestial flame, symbolized by a lioness. She simultaneously manifests both the creative and destructive aspects of *neter*. Sekhmet is usually portrayed as a woman with the head of a lioness and is associated with Wadjet, as she bears the Uraeus. Sometimes she is depicted holding a knife in her right hand.

Sekhmet's son Nefertum can also be depicted as a human with the head of a lion, however, he is usually portrayed as a man with a lotus flower upon his head. In the *Pyramid Texts* it is written that "Unas appears as Nefertum, the lotus at the nose of Re, as he comes out of the Horizon every day, and at the sight of which the gods purify themselves" (*PT* 266). During the period of the New Kingdom, Imhotep replaced Nefertum in the theological triad of Memphis. Imhotep is also referred to as the son of Tatenen (a deity of the primordial Earth) who grants life to humans, manages the change of

---

16. Howard C. Kee, "Self-Definition in the Asclepius Cult", in *Jewish and Christian Self-Definition, vol.III: Self-Definition in the Graeco-Roman World*, ed. by Ben F. Meyer, E. P. Sanders, SCM Press, 1982, p. 133.

seasons, heals the sick and helps childless couples. He bears the likeness of Thoth.

As a historical figure, Imhotep is mentioned in the inscription at the base of the statue of Djoser, a pharaoh of the Third Dynasty to whom Imhotep served as a chancellor. Here, he is described as the builder, sculptor and maker of stone vases, the overseer of masons and painters, the royal chancellor, the ruler of the great mansion and the greatest of seers. He is also referred to as the high priest of Ra and "First After the King of Upper Egypt". It is apparent that Imhotep is the architect of Djoser's pyramid, the earliest large-scale stone building in Egypt. As the time went by, the reputation of this legendary architect and physician only grew, resulting in his deification during the period of the New Kingdom, equating him with Asclepius himself. A tomb in Thebes from the time of Amenhotep III bears an inscription that says: "May the water in the cup of any scribe [be offered in libation] to your *ka*, Imhotep."[17]

Eventually, Imhotep becomes the patron of scribes, getting canonized rites. The works of Imhotep and Djedefhor, the son of Pharaoh Khufu, become a part of the wisdom literature tradition. Unfortunately, the works of Imhotep did not survive. Still, the name of Imhotep is included on the lists of notable people like pharaohs and high priests of Memphis. Various sources (like Turin Papyrus of Kings) call him the inventor of stone block construction and an expert in hieroglyphs. However, according to D. Wildung, even though Manetho, the author of the *Aegyptiaca*, attributes all these achievements to Djoser, it does not diminish the importance of Imhotep, as the pharaoh personifies all the accomplishments achieved during his reign.[18]

In the period of the New Kingdom, Imhotep was referred to as a descendant of gods. Various statues depicted him

---

17. Dietrich Wildung, *Egyptian Saints. Deification in Pharaonic Egypt*, New York University Press, New York, 1977, p. 34.

18. *Ibid.*, p. 38.

as a man with very short hair or a cap, sitting on a chair or a pedestal. On his lap he has a scroll with the infamous ritualistic words: "May the water in the cup of any scribe [be offered in libation] to your ka, Imhotep". This image of the son of Ptah reading a scroll is regarded as a symbol of wisdom, especially when keeping in mind that the name of Imhotep is related to wisdom literature and the concept of intellectual inspiration. The cap of Imhotep bears a striking resemblance to the one worn by Ptah, and thus symbolizes his connection with the paternal Intellect, while the skirt represents his priest status.

During the Thirtieth Dynasty, there existed a triad of Apis-Osiris, Imhotep and Ptah. The depiction of Imhotep changes, as he is now portrayed with additional sacred attributes—the symbol of *ankh* and a staff. The high priest is venerated as a physician, the giver of life, and a mediator between the earthly and sacred realms. The cult of Imhotep is prominent among noblemen and intellectuals like physicians, scribes and priests. It is this version of Imhotep—a sage, sacred physician, astronomer and master of magic—that gets identified with Asclepius and becomes a character of early Hermetic literature.

· AMON AND AGATHODAEMON ·

Amon (Amun, Ammon, or Amen), the anthropomorphized patron of Thebes, is another character of Hermetic literature. At the beginning of the New Kingdom, he becomes known as a creator deity whose manifestations create the visible world, however, euhemeristic hermeneutics transforms him into an earthly ruler. Plato states in *Phaedrus* that it was Thoth who revealed to Amon the secrets of his sacred wisdom and the art of hieroglyphs (*Phaedr.* 274d.). In his true form, Amon is *Amun-Ra nesu neteru* (*Amonrasonther* in Greek)—the ruler of the gods, recognized as the one true god not only in Thebes, but also in all of Egypt after the defeat of the Hyksos.

In a way, Amon can be viewed as an all-permeating spirit or the breath of life (*suh en ankh*, or *pneuma* in Greek). That is why K. Sethe depicts him as a demiurgic wind, blowing above the waters of Nun, in an attempt to identify him as the spirit of the Biblical God, who hovers above the primordial waters and whose "breath" becomes the Holy Spirit, a separate entity in the Christian tradition, just like the eye of the Sun god (Amun-Ra) becomes a separate goddess in the Egyptian tradition.[19]

In the literal sense, the word "Amun" means "the hidden one", "invisible", "mysterious of form". In the Hermopolitan theology, Amun is one of the four primordial deities, referred to as "the one who hides his name". Amun's children do not know the name of their father, who dwells in the depths of Nun. However, Amun emerges from the primordial waters in the form of *ba*—the sacred ram, or the representation of Soul. The kind of ram that represents Amun is called *ovis platyura aegyptiaca*, which replaced *ovis longipes aegyptiaca*, a now extinct wild barbary sheep, during the period of the Middle Kingdom. Amun is also symbolized by a sacred goose, but the Amun that dwells in the waters of Nun is depicted as a primordial Serpent. In Thebes, this creature of darkness is called Kematef ("he who has fulfilled his time"), while in Hermopolis he is called the Son of the Earth. It is the first manifestation of the highest deity, an archetypal image of God, described in the *Pyramid Texts* as follows:

> N. is the pouring down of rain; he came forth as the coming into being of water; for he is the Nhb-k3.w-serpent with the many coils; N. is the scribe of the divine book, who says what is and causes to exist what is not. (*PT* 1146)

The Spirit of God, who manifests himself in the form of a serpent, grants life (*ka*) to all his creations and distributes all

---

19. K. Sethe, *Amun und die Acht Urgotter von Hermopolis*, Berlin, 1929, in E. A. Wallis Budge, *The Gods of the Egyptians*, p. 170.

the fundamental attributes of existence. Wrapped around his own body and thus self-contained, he utters the all-creating Word. In the *Coffin Texts*, this Serpent calls himself the most powerful of all the gods: "Sovereign of the Powers, [...] Lord of all that is his" (*CT* IV.321). Various mythical images intertwine in these depictions of the primordial Serpent, who is associated with Atum, the creator of Shu and Tefnut, the first sacred pair. The coils of the Serpent represent infinity and boundlessness (*apeiron*) but, simultaneously, set the boundaries (*peras*), or establish different levels of manifestation. At the centre of the coils of the Serpent, who is equivalent to the Scribe of the sacred book of archetypes, echoes the demiurgical Word (*Logos*).

As mentioned earlier, this Serpent, or *Nehebkau*, is referred to as "the hidden one" and "invisible" (i.e. Amun), the provider of spirit, vitality and being. He is depicted as a two-headed snake next to the symbol of *ankh*. Manifesting in the form of Atum, he "slays" his former, invisible self and creates the world of manifestations, i.e. the primordial mound, represented by the city of Hermopolis. Nevertheless, the Universe—or the city of Thoth—is still encircled by the Son of the Earth—a Serpent eating its own tail. It is the Hermetic *Ouroboros*, reiterated on all the levels of being.

Eventually, Atum (i.e. the world of noetic, psychical and physical manifestations) must return to the primeval depths, thus becoming the invisible and inexpressible One, symbolized by the transcendental aspect of the primordial Serpent. On the level of the Soul of the World (speaking in Neoplatonist terms), the cosmic Snake coils around Duat, the realm of the dead.

Ouroboros is the symbol of the integrity of the cosmos, sacred unity and eternity. In a metaphysical sense, the beginning and the end become one, while transitional levels of being advance in spiral cycles. In Greek and Egyptian alchemy, it symbolizes the cosmogonic Egg, which contains all the manifestations of being (or its archetypes). This Egg is also referred to as the philosopher's stone.

The image of a winged serpent is also related to Agatho-daemon (*Agathos Daimon*, good god/fortune), a spirit worshipped in Hellenistic Egypt that later became a dramatic character in Hermetic literary works and a spiritual patron. In one of Hermetic dialogues, Osiris speaks to the "thrice-great" Agathodaemon, inquiring the reason behind the rising of the Sun. In the surviving excerpts of *Kore Kosmou*, Isis tells Horus about the wisdom chain of alchemy and Hermetic philosophy: "Give heed, my son Horus, for you shall hear secret doctrine, of which our forefather Kamephis was the first teacher. It so befell that Hermes heard this teaching from Kamephis, the eldest of our race. I heard it from Hermes, the writer of records, at the time when he initiated me in the Black Rites, and you shall hear it now from me..." (*SH* IV.8)

Kamephis is the Greek transcription of the Egyptian *Chnoubis*. It is a hermaphroditic serpent that gave birth to itself (*autogennetos*), a demiurge of the noetic cosmos equated to Min, the Egyptian god of fertility depicted with an erect phallus akin to Greek herma sculptures. Damascius interprets Kamephis as a demiurgic triad of primordial principles (*archai*). The first component of this triad comes from the diad of Water and Sand, the second component—from the first one, while the third—from the second one. Damascius writes:

> Of the Egyptian doctrines Eudemus gives us no accurate information. But the Egyptian philosophers, who are resident among us, have explained their occult truth, having obtained it from certain Egyptian discourses. According to them, then it appears to be this. The One principle of the Universe is celebrated as Unknown Darkness, and this three-times pronounced as such: and the Two principles are Water and Sand, according to Heraïscus; but according to Asclepiades, who is the more ancient of the two, Sand and Water, from whom, and next in succession after them, is generated the first Kamephis, and from this a second, and from this again a third, which, they affirm, completes the whole Intelligible

distribution. Such is the system of Asclepiades. But the more modern Heraïscus says that the third, who is named Kamephis from his father and grandfather, is the Sun, equivalent in this case to the Intelligible Mind. But greater accuracy upon the subject can only be obtained from these authors themselves. It must be observed, however, with regard to the Egyptians, that they are often wont to distribute subsistence according to union, as when they divide the Intelligible into the individualities of a multitude of gods, as may be learnt from their own writings by those who will examine them: I refer particularly to the commentary of Heraïscus upon the Egyptian doctrine addressed to Proclus the philosopher alone, and to the concordance of the Egyptian writers, begun by Asclepiades and addressed to the other Theologists. (*De principiis* I.323.18–324.15)

According to Damascius, three Kamepheis comprise a noetic triad, characteristic to the theology of late Neoplatonism. Certain researchers speculate that Kamephis is not only an equivalent to Amun or Min, but also a title for priests or an epithet for various gods (Ptah, for example).

In *Kore Kosmou* it is written that Hermes obtains his secret knowledge (*gnosis*) from Kamephis. However, the literary work does not talk about specific individuals—it rather alludes to archetypes, personified by the collective memory. These archetypes reflect the true or imaginative genealogy of the wisdom tradition. Kamephis is thought to be connected to Khnum, the ram-headed creator of the World who made humans from clay and who is sometimes referred to as the "father of the fathers".

J. Lindsay explains the connection between the god Khum and the image of a serpent:

The magical gems do much to fill out the picture. Here indeed we do find the god Khnum linked with a serpent: On one side we see a bearded serpent coiled on the right; on the reverse is an inscription *Chnoubis Nabis Bienout*—a corruption of a common formula, *Chnoubis Naabis Biennouth*, which is normally met in connection with the bearded serpent. Chnoubis is a late variant of Khnum. *Naabis* seems linked with the Egyptian root, *nhp*, which denotes the potter's-wheel or else an hypostasis of the god existing independently or under the form *Khnum-Nph*. *Biennouth* corresponds to an Egyptian term meaning the soul-of-the-god. This name suits Khnum in particular, since the Egyptian for Ram was homophonous with the word for the Soul. The Egyptians liked this sort of serious pun, which was felt to reveal hidden connections; here they built up theological subtleties on the similarity of sound, making the Divine Ram the Soul of the Gods and associating the four forms he assumed in his four sanctuaries with the four great elementary gods. Thus we find that each term of the inscription on the gem links with Khnum.[20]

He later describes a gem with a fusion of Hermes-Thoth-Agathodaemon:

We also find Thoth brought in. A haematite gem shows a deity with neck and head of ibis and crowned snake; on the reverse the lad palindrome, Chnoubis, and the words pesse pesse, showing that amulet was for stomach-troubles. The odd figure may be taken as a fusion of Hermes-Thoth and Agathodaimon, as found also in the inscription Thaut Psae on an amulet reverse, with Thoth's ibis on the other side, holding a caduceus under its wing and bearing on its head a tiny figure of Harpokrates.[21]

Various gems depict Agathodaemon as a bearded primordial Serpent wearing the crown of *pschent*, which symbolizes power. Sometimes he is portrayed as a lion-headed snake with seven solar rays beaming out of its head. Next to the rays there

20. Jack Lindsay, *The Origins of Alchemy in Graeco-Roman Egypt*, Barnes and Noble, New York, 1970, p. 269.
21. *Ibid.*, p. 312.

are written the seven vowels of the Greek alphabet (representing seven planets), the combinations of which comprise the secret names of the gods, or the theurgical mantras, chanted during sacred rituals, thus echoing the demiurgical Word. The lion symbolizes the solar Intellect and its power (*sekhmet*), while the snake is an embodiment of *heka*—the cosmic magic. Hermetic texts unambiguously refer to Agathodaemon as the universal Intellect (*Nous*). Olympiodorus, a fifth-century alchemist, wrote:

> Some of the natural philosophers bring back the argument on the elements to the *arche*, in view of the fact that *archai* are something more general than the elements. Indeed the first principle resumes the whole of the art. Thus Agathodaimon, placing the *arche* in the end and the end in the *arche*, wants it to be the serpent Ouroboros... [...] Agathodaimon, what is he? Some hold he is an ancient, one of the oldest persons who occupied themselves with philosophy in Egypt. Others have called him the Heavens—perhaps because the serpent is the image of the universe. Indeed certain Egyptian hieroglyphics, wanting to trace the world on obelisks or express it in sacred characters, show the serpent Ouroboros. His body is constellated with stars. That is, I've been told, because he is the *arche*.[22]

Sometimes, domestic snakes were kept as a tribute to Agathodaemon. They were regarded as house guardians. In this way, Agathodaemon is a guardian angel, a spirit, a mystical guide and the main principle of alchemical transformations. In the form of Kamephis, he is the Demiurge and patron of the world, while Agathodaemon and Hermes, according to the Arab tradition, are the founders of Harranian alchemy and the harbingers of the Sabian wisdom tradition.

---

22. *Ibid.*, p. 362.

· HERMES TRISMEGISTUS IN THE HELLENISTIC PERIOD ·

The merging of Thoth and Hermes is a result of a long and complicated process of the relationship between Egyptian and Greek cultures, which reached its peak during the Late Period of Egypt. This period is characterized not only by direct contact with various cultures (Assyrian, Persian, Greek, etc.), but also by the idealization of the Egyptian past and a rapid development of symbolic-esoteric discourse (modelled in the example of metaphysical hermeneutics), thus emphasizing the superiority of Egyptian wisdom and the power of theurgical transformation. However, in the context of Hellenistic culture, the superiority of the Egyptian wisdom is often emphasized by reinterpreting it through the lens of Hellenic philosophy. Thus, Thoth becomes the universal symbol of the heritage of ancient priests and scribes in the form of Hermes.

Since the third century BC, Hermes' name obtains a honorific of Thoth translated from the Egyptian language—*megistos kai megistos theos megas*. However, an abbreviation of this phrase—Trismegistus—becomes canonized only during the period of the Roman Empire. The popularity of Thoth-Hermes among Egyptians and Hellens is proven by various inscriptions left by Egyptian, Roman and Greek pilgrims on the walls of the temple of Paotnuphis. The archive of Memphis, dated back to the second century BC, also testifies the popularity of Hermes. One of the papyri of this archive, *the Art of Eudoxus*, calls itself "the Oracles of Hermes". According to D. J. Thompson, it is the "earliest illustrated scientific work to have survived from antiquity."[23] As Thoth-Hermes was regarded as the symbol of all scientific accomplishments and the author of all sacred rituals, religious recitations, magical formulas and iconography, many esoteric wisdom traditions operated under his name.

---

23. D. J. Thompson, *Memphis under the Ptolemies*, Princeton University Press, Princeton, 1988, p. 252–262.

The cultural prowess of Hermes Trismegistus in Hellenistic Egypt was so immense that even Jewish intellectuals borrowed certain elements of it. Artapanus of Alexandria, a historian who lived during the second century BC, identified Hermes with Moses, claiming that it was he who taught philosophy to the Egyptians, invented the hieroglyphs, divided the country into nomes, began building ships and making weapons. Thus, the true hero of the Egyptian culture was Moses, not Hermes. However, even though this opinion was supported by certain scholars, it remained somewhat debatable.

The Hellenic Hermes is a multifaceted figure, composed of diverse mythical and philosophical elements. Even the eloquence of Paul the Apostle is compared to the one of Hermes, who was referred to as *Hermes Logios* and renowned as the patron of ritualistic diction, rhetorics and sophistic dialectics. However, the most important aspect of him is the fact that he is *hermeneus*, i.e. the hermeneut of the divine and the founder of allegorical interpretation, able to interpret symbols and convey the religious-philosophical terminology from one culture into another. A hermeneut allows the communication between different cultures, explains the will of the gods to humanity and reveals the true meaning (*huponoia*) of signs (*semeia*) and esoteric riddles (*ainigmata*).

Hermes also plays an important role in Stoic theology, as he is regarded as an immanent world-creating *logos* that justifies the logic of existence. However, the educated Greeks, strongly affected by rationalism, do not call Hermes Trismegistus a god, and thus emphasize his humanity. He is not a deity *per se*, but a human sage from the ancient times, not a messenger of the gods, but a talented hermeneut. In this regard, the Greek and Egyptian points of view differ radically, and that is why there appear two Hermes—one is similar to a human while the other resembles a god. The Greeks often ignored and rejected the Egyptian traits of Hermes Trismegistus, turning his divine traits into human qualities. Thus, Plato does not know if he should refer to Thoth as a god or (succumbing to the clutches of rationalism) a divine human (*Phileb.* 18.b).

It is not surprising that Greek literary works of philosophical Hermeticism depict Hermes as a mortal (though
extraordinary) human, who learns cosmological knowledge
(*gnosis*) through sacred revelations and who becomes immortal through philosophical cleansing (*katharsis*) and spiritual
improvement. However, more ancient sources of Egyptian
Hermetic literature unambiguously refer to Hermes as a god.
G. Fowden writes:

> According to *Kore kosmou*, Hermes was a god who succeeded
> in understanding the mysteries of the heavens, and revealed
> them by inscribing them in sacred books, which he then hid
> here on earth, intending that they should be searched for
> by future generations, but found only by the fully worthy.
> Having finished his task he returned to the celestial abode of
> the gods; but he left behind a successor, Tat, together with
> Asclepius-Imouthes and others not named. This plurality
> of authorities in Hermetism is much noticed in modern ac-
> counts of the subject; but since the Hermetists themselves in-
> sisted on it, we ignore it at our peril.[24]

The Hellenistic Hermetic literature that emerged during
the Ptolemaic Period and the first centuries of the Roman
rule might have been based on early Egyptian concepts (and
thus presented its truths as the revelation of the gods); however, its ideas accommodate the philosophical context of
Platonism, Pythagoreanism and Stoicism and are expressed
through the terminology of Greek philosophy, indirectly appealing to the cosmology of Plato's *Timaeus* and various concepts of Hellenistic science (astrology, eschatology, etc.). In
addition, the Pythagorean concept of philosophy becomes
the standard and somewhat universal paradigm. Nevertheless,
Hermetic dialogues are not just a replica of Plato's dialogues,

---

24. Garth Fowden, *The Egyptian Hermes. A Historical Approach to the Late
Pagan Mind*. Princeton University Press, 1993, p. 33.

as Plato himself might have referred to the examples of the Egyptian wisdom literature, written in the form of dialogue.

Despite all the Greek terms and concepts (shared by the whole civilized world at that time), the environment and spirit of the Hermetic dialogues are unmistakably Egyptian. Besides Hermes Trismegistus, the dramatic characters of the mentioned dialogues include Asclepius (Imhotep), Agathodaemon, Amon, Isis, Horus, Poimandres and Tat. It seems that Tat might be a variation of Thoth's name (i.e., *Pap. Graec. Mag.* VII.551-557). Eventually, Tat becomes the physical and spiritual son of Thoth. This dual figure of Thoth is reflected by Arabic Hermetic literature where Tat becomes Sabi ibn Idris, the son of the prophet Idris.

The tradition of Hellenistic philosophy also mentions two Hermes. Synesius, a fifth-century Neoplatonist, claims that Egyptians portray Hermes as a double entity, depicting a young and an old man next to each other. The first one symbolizes courage while the other one—wisdom (*De regno* 7; *De providentia* I.2). Likewise, here are two Asclepiuses (*Ascl.* 37): one of them is the Greek Asclepius, the other the Egyptian Imouthes, or the son of Hephaestus (i.e. Ptah). Meanwhile, the young Hermes often becomes the grandson of the old one. In the work *Asclepius: The Perfect Discourse,* its supposed author Hermes Trismegistus mentions the tomb of his grandfather Hermes, which is situated in Hermopolis—his *patria,* also referred to as the city of Hermes. In this case, the first Hermes is the Egyptian god Thoth, while the other—a sage, whose concept is much closer to the euhemeristic Hellenic mentality. In addition, Hermes can be regarded as a spiritual title, as a symbol of the sacred Intellect embodied by the figure of the "teacher-father", or as a level of spiritual realization. If so, one can become Hermes in the same way one can become Buddha.

The tradition of the *Greek Magical Papyri* emphasizes the Egyptian attributes of Hermes Trismegistus more than the Hermetic dialogues. This tradition, associated with theurgic rituals, spells and syncretic magic, is barely related to philosophical Hermeticism. However, we cannot be certainly sure about that, keeping in mind the wide variety of schools of thought in ancient Rome, as well as their openness to cultural influence. The Magical Papyri not only refer to Hermes as Trismegistus (*trismegas, trismegistos*), but also associate him with Tat (*Thath: Pap. Graec. Mag.* VII.511-557). However, here, Hermes is more similar to Thoth and Heka, the god of magic. He is the creator of Heaven and Earth, an all-powerful ruler of the world (*pantokrator, kosmokrator*), responsible for justice and the faith of both the whole universe and the individual. Together with Hecate and Selene (the Moon), Hermes is the Lord of the Night, aware of everything that happens under the Sky or underneath the Earth. Thus, he can send prophetic dreams or even manifest himself as the ruler of cosmic magic. From the microcosmic point of view, he dwells in the heart of every human (*enkardios*), and that is why a mage attempts to reveal the spark of divinity that exists within himself—to wake Hermes up and to merge with him, thus becoming a master of demiurgic magic: "I know you, Hermes, and you know me. I am you, and you are me."[25] According to G. Fowden, such self-identification with a god is a trait of the ancient Egyptian culture.[26]

· THE CONNECTION BETWEEN THE GREEK AND EGYPTIAN CULTURES ·

Under Ptolemaic and Roman rule, the culture of Egypt was a blend of the Hellenic and Egyptian traditions. Any Egyptian pursuing a higher social status had to be able to speak Greek and be familiar with the culture of his conquerors, who then had full political power. However, despite the influence of the cosmopolitan Alexandria (one of the biggest cultural centres of Hellenic literature and philosophy in Antiquity, often not even considered a part of Egypt), the Egyptian spirit was still domi-

---

25. *Ibid.*, p. 26.
26. *Idem.*

nant in the deeper parts of the country. The need to emphasize the Egyptian identity is reflected by Hermetic literature
and the political and religious predictions, targeted against
the Greek government. Despite this animosity, the Greek language remained official while the Hellenic culture and philosophy were held as an example for the educated nobility.

At first, merging the Egyptian and Hellenic cultures was
difficult. Before Egyptian temples and their priest communities were affected by economic constraints that radically limited their independence and influence (which happened after
the spread of Christianity), Egyptian priests tried to emphasize the superiority of their own esoteric wisdom and symbolic hermeneutics over Hellenic philosophy. The Alexandrian
cult of Serapis was of little interest to the priests and people who lived further in the country, as Serapis was merely
a Greek god and his iconography deviated from the traditional Canon. As a city, Alexandria had little connection to
Egypt and thus was officially referred to as *Alexandreia he pros
Aigyptou*—Alexandria that is located near Egypt.

Memphis represented the tendencies of Egyptian culture.
Here, Serapis was worshipped as Osor-Hapis and Asar-Hapis,
i.e. as a combination of Osiris and Hapis (or Apis), the sacred
bull. The procession path to the serapeum of Memphis was
surrounded by classical Hellenic statues of poets and philosophers (including Plato and Socrates), however, the temple's
interior, its rituals and priests were exceptionally Egyptian.
On the contrary, the rituals of the Serapeum of Alexandria
were mainly Greek.

During the Ptolemaic era, a series of predictions were popular among the Egyptians. These were written in the example
of genre models known since the Middle Kingdom. *The Oracle
of the Potter* (i.e. the prophecy of Khnum, the god of the potter's wheel) proclaimed that the "belt wearers", i.e. Hellens,
were the followers of Typhon (which was the Greek name for
Set, the enemy of Horus) and that they would eventually be
responsible for their own destruction. Then, Agathodaemon
would leave their city (Alexandria) and move to the pious
Memphis. The city of foreign sinners would turn into a desert.

The sinners themselves would disappear, and their city would turn into a desert. Then, Egypt would be reborn, and the glory of the old days would return.

The famous prophecy of Hermes (*Ascl.* 24b–25) also belongs to this traditional genre. It claims that someday, a time will come when the gods will leave Egypt and chaos will ensue in the form of violence of the outsiders. The apologists of Christianity reinterpreted this prophecy as a testament of the triumph of their religion; however, it is unlikely that the mentioned text is a direct reference to the fourth-century persecution of "pagans". Since the first Intermediate Period (2150–2040 BC), there had been a lot of discussions about cosmic chaos and the restoration of *maat*, i.e. the return of the Golden Age, which occurred periodically. Texts like this prophecy can be tailored according to the ever-changing historical circumstances because they describe myths and archetypal models instead of time-specific realia. The tragedy of Egypt is merely a temporary cosmological episode in the historical shift between "night" and "day".

Hermetic mythology longs for the Golden Age of Egypt despite its Hellenistic nature, thus reflecting the situation of Egypt at that time. However, Hermeticists claimed that they were merely translating Egyptian texts into Greek or conveying the doctrines, written in hieroglyphs, into philosophical terminology, even though the Greek language was not suitable for this purpose. That is because words maintain their theurgical power only when they are uttered in the holy Egyptian language or depicted in hieroglyphs.

Neoplatonist Iamblichus also claimed that Greek Hermetic literature was merely a philosophical reinterpretation of Egyptian texts. He indicated that the Egyptian priest Bitus translated some of the Thoth's works (*De myster.* VIII.5; X.7), which he had found in the temple of the city of Sais, into the philosophical Greek language. Iamblichus stated that Plato and Pythagoras had studied Hermes' (or Thoth's) stelas with the help of Egyptian priests.

One text of the Oxyrhynchus Papyri contains fragments of an unfinished translation into Greek of an aretalogy about

Asclepius-Imouthes. The text demonstrates that Egyptians attempted to propagate and universalize their religious ideas. The translator of the work admits that he is not going to translate this Egyptian text word by word, but rather adapt it for the Greek-speaking public, i.e. remove any mythological details foreign to the Hellenic culture. According to G. Fowden, the fact that the work is written as an aretalogy is a proof that the text emerged in a cultural environment similar to Hermeticism.[27] It also implies that the tradition of philosophical Hermeticism is merely one of the many trends of adapting and propagating Hellenised Egyptian wisdom. In addition, many intellectuals of Antiquity were firmly convinced that Platonic philosophy had originated in Egypt, and that is why Hermeticists could openly claim the ideas of Pythagoreanism and Platonism as their own. A fragment of a third-century astrological dialogue between Plato and Egyptian priests indicates the interest in these topics at that time.

According to Plutarch, Pythagoras was inspired by the symbolism and the form of expression of Egyptian priests, and thus he conveyed his teachings in enigmatic statements, which can be compared to Egyptian hieroglyphs (*De Iside et Osiride* 10). Chaeremon, a Stoic philosopher from Alexandria, was of a similar opinion and depicted Egyptian priests as sacred sages and Pythagoreans who practiced philosophical ascesis. All of this sheds some light on the cultural context of the emergence of Hermetic literature, built on the authority of a universalized version of Thoth—Hermes Trismegistus.

· THE WISDOM BOOKS OF THOTH ·

A lot of authors of Antiquity wrote about the wisdom of Thoth-Hermes who had presumably etched it onto obelisks and stelas. According to Diodorus Siculus, Hermes not only

---

27. *Idem.*

gave names to nameless objects, but also granted humans with a shared language—an intellectual discourse open to translation and interpretation. He invented the alphabet, established sacrificial rituals and discovered the music of the spheres. Inspired by the three seasons of the Egyptian calendar, he invented the three-stringed lyre whose tones corresponded to summer, winter and spring. He taught Hellens the art of interpretation (*hermeneia*), and that is why he was called Hermes. He became the scribe and the closest adviser of Osiris (*Bibl. hist.* I.16). Only priests, sages and the followers of Hermes can understand and correctly interpret the sacred symbols, the hieroglyphs of the stelas and all the esoteric wisdom of Thoth-Hermes. As stated by Iamblichus, Pythagoras and Plato were among the sages who studied Hermes' stelas, which means that all the tradition of Platonism represents a "modern" variant of the perennial wisdom.

Certain Arab authors believed that Hermes built the Egyptian pyramids and hid various instructions on alchemy and theurgic sciences inside them. M. Psellos, a Byzantine author, claimed that Plato travelled to Egypt in order to study these texts. A Persian astrologer Abu Ma'shar writes:

He was the first to prophesy the coming of the Flood and saw that heavenly plague by water and fire threatened the Earth. His domicile was Sa'id of Egypt, which he selected for himself, and he built there the sanctuaries of the Pyramids and the temple towns. It was because of his fear that wisdom might be lost that he built the temples, namely, the mountain known as al-Barba, the temple of Akhmim (Panopolis), engraved on their walls drawings of all techniques and their technicians, made pictures of all the working-tools of craftsmen, and by inscriptions indicated the essence of the sciences for the benefit of those who were to come after him. In doing so, he was guided by the desire of preserving sciences for later generations and by fear that its trace might disappear from the world.[28]

---

28. Jack Lindsay, *The Origins of Alchemy in Graeco-Roman Egypt*, p. 173.

Various arts and crafts manuals and the texts of esoteric wisdom were concealed from the public eye, and were often buried with their authors. That is why it is unsurprising that tombs became the sources of sacred wisdom. People came there looking for philosophical teachings and alchemical instructions. For example, one tomb of two mages in Thebes contained papyrus scrolls about magic, metals and textile. Similar texts (for example, *Leyden Papyrus V*) talk about the symbolic titles of plants and minerals, magical god images and coded talismans that are made in a way so that those who are unworthy would not obtain magical powers.[29]

Some legends say that even philosophers broke into the tombs of ancient sages. For example, Democritus is said to have robbed the tomb of Dardan in pursuit of finding his books on magic. Books on esoteric wisdom are claimed to be found inside the tombs of Hermes Trismegistus, Alexander the Great, Cleopatra and various kings. A lot of alchemists and astrologers announce their own writings as revelations, copied from ancient pillars or Egyptian temples. Magical papyri contain quotes like this: "[To Hermes:] Your true name has been inscribed on the sacred stele in the shrine at Hermopolis where your birth is". Statements like these allude to ancient Egypt, thus validating contemporary doctrines that retrospectively refer to the archetypal Golden Age. Oftentimes they have little to do with the authentic tradition of ancient Egyptian scribes, however, occasionally they are based on true elements of this tradition. The sacred literature of ancient Egypt (in the wide sense of the word) was created, edited, commented and rewritten by priests—the scribes (*hierogrammateis*) of the House of Life (*per ankh*). The House of Life is the residence of the scribes, which symbolizes the whole cosmos and which can be identified as the body of Osiris-Ra. It is also a shrine, a school and a library.

We can form an opinion about the contents of the books kept in the vaults of temples thanks to a catalogue found in

---

29. *Ibid.*, p. 124.

the temple of Horus at Edfu. In the library of this temple, whose construction was finished in 57 BC, there is a two-part list of books carved on the walls, which was originally composed in 140–124 BC. The first part mentions liturgical and mythological works, the second lists scientific and magical texts; however, modern classification might not be appropriate here. The catalogue mentions Thoth as the god of Ra's manifestations. The second part reads as follows:

> I bring to you [Horus] caskets containing excellent mysteries, to wit the choices of the Emanations of Re [i.e. holy books].
> Book of the temple-inventory.
> Book of the threatening [of Seth?]
> Book containing all the writings about the struggle [of Horus against Seth?]
> Book of the plan of the temple.
> Book of the guardians of the temple.
> Specification for the painting of a wall.
> Book of the protection of the body.
> Book of the protection of the king in his house.
> Spells for the averting of the evil eye.
> Knowledge of the recurrence of the two stars [sun and moon].
> Control over the recurrence of the stars.
> Enumeration of all places, and knowledge of what is to be found in them.
> All the protective formulae for the departure of Your Majesty from your temple for your feasts.[30]

Clement of Alexandria, a Christian theologian and philosopher, mentions forty-two books by Thoth when describing a procession of priests, during which these books are carried in a hierarchical order. Their topics often correspond to the books from the catalogue of the temple of Edfu. According

---

30. Garth Fowden, *The Egyptian Hermes. A Historical Approach to the Late Pagan Mind*, p. 57–58

to Clement of Alexandria, thirty-six books of the mentioned forty-two contain the whole Egyptian philosophy (*Strom.* VI.4.35ff). A Greek geographer and philosopher Strabo, when talking about Theban astronomers and philosophers, claims that all the wisdom of this kind is attributed to Hermes (*Geogr.* XVII.1.46). Certain writers believe Hermes to be the author of thousands if not hundreds of thousands of books, i.e. nearly the entire religious-scientific Egyptian literature that reached the modern world only in small fragments. However, even if these numbers are an exaggeration, the scope of the works was still impressive. Also, it is well known that a lot of these books were never made public.

One of the main functions of Egyptian priests was the protection of truth, justice and cosmic harmony (*maat*) by all means necessary, including rigorous rituals that maintained the communities of gods and humans. The sacred books contained liturgical words, theological commentaries and descriptions of cyclical rituals, all of which were a huge part of the sacred wisdom tradition. These kinds of books guaranteed the preservation of cosmic order in both literal and figurative sense. Thoth's writings were known for sacramental effectiveness, liturgically reflecting cosmogonic and demiurgical realities, especially when keeping in mind that Thoth himself was responsible for uttering and writing down the words that created the world. The universe is a text written in his hieroglyphs. It embodies the thoughts of the sacred Intelligence, or the heart of Ra. In this regard, all the rites, liturgy, choreography, iconography, symbolism and symbolic hermeneutics are Thoth's established realities that reflect the eternal paradigms. These are not concepts of humans, but rather actions intended for the gods, imitated by priests, through whom Thoth speaks. Even the spells of magical papyri are uttered not by a mage, but rather by the mask of a god worn by him. It is as if the mage impersonates a god or attempts to temporarily become one.

In this theatre of metaphysical dramaturgy, Thoth's books (i.e. all the hieroglyphical texts) play a theurgical role, especially when keeping in mind that hieroglyphs are *medu neter*—

words of nature, or the manifestations of demiurgic Intellect, embedded into the form of earthly rituals. However, the books written by priests were not limited to theology, liturgy and theurgical rites—the topics included medicine, anatomy, geography, botany, mineralogy, etc. As the culture of ancient Egypt regarded the natural world as a world of sacred manifestations, all the elements of being were supernatural; thus, every natural phenomenon was permeated by the light of its corresponding primordial principle. To reveal this light is the goal of sacred hermeneutics.

The papyri found in Faiyum confirm that certain ancient texts were rewritten and translated during the times of the Roman Empire,[31] while the papyri of Tebtunis explore cosmology, astrology, magic, dream interpretation, medicine, temple administration and liturgy. Among them there are examples of wisdom literature (moral advice) written in hieroglyphs, hieratic script, demotic script and in Greek.[32] Some of the texts are thematically related to the works mentioned in the catalogue of Edfu. G. Fowden comments on certain works:

> The other three papyri in the group provide unique examples of Egyptian speculative literature. They show a strong interest in cosmogony and the understanding of the powers latent in the material world, and make several references to the god Thoth and his writings—the situation they envisage is one in which a teacher, perhaps Thoth himself, instructs a pupil in divine wisdom, apparently in the setting of a temple. In the text, we find a reference to the *hp n ntr*, the "law of the god". The god with whom the concept *hp* was most commonly associated was Thoth. [...] The assumption behind all

---

31. E. A. E. Reymond (ed.), *From the Contents of the Libraries of the Suchos Temples in the Fayyum II: From Ancient Egyptian Hermetic Writings*, Vienna, 1977.
32. Garth Fowden, *The Egyptian Hermes. A Historical Approach to the Late Pagan Mind*, p. 26.

these texts is that knowledge comes from the gods, and in particular from Thoth, and that its possession endows one with power which (by implication) is analogous to that of the gods themselves.[33]

Egyptian texts emphasize that knowledge is bestowed by the gods. The mentioned papyri from the city of Faiyum contain the phrase *mre rhw*, or *mere rekhu*—"pursuing wisdom".[34] It seems that it is a direct equivalent of the Greek word *philosophia*. Thus, Thoth is the patron and the archetype of philosophy—its beginning, middle and end.

· THE SACRED HERMENEUTICS OF ANCIENT EGYPT ·

The Egyptian Thoth is not only the scribe of the gods, but also a hermeneut. Even though this aspect of Egyptian culture has not been sufficiently explored, it seems that the Hellens took a lot of inspiration from it. Keeping in mind the importance of the sacred name (*ren*) in the Egyptian religion, we can see this concept's connection with Plato's *Cratylus*, the topics of Stoicism, as well as the symbolic hermeneutics of Neoplatonism. This name (*ren*) is the most important part of metaphysics and theology. Deities manifest themselves through their names and cult images, and that is why the names of all objects are the masks of *neteru* (spirits, gods). The name of a god can be seen as his or her image that comprises all the theology, mythology and history into a single theurgical entity. In this regard, a catalogue of sacred names and a list of attributes and epithets are more important than mythology with a literary plot.

If a name is interpreted correctly, it can reveal the essence of an object. Meanwhile, a depiction of an object or a person can be regarded as their visual archetypal form. From this

---

33. *Idem.*
34. *Idem.*

point of view, speech is a picture that depicts the archetypal contours of being. Thus, language is a cult action: to name something is to grant it existence as well as a meaning that corresponds with a certain category.

J. Assmann states that in Egyptian hymns, a combination of names is interpreted by determining the connection between 1) a god, 2) an action and 3) a visible object, which usually belongs to a religious cult and can be interpreted as the name of a god.[35] However, sometimes it is difficult to understand these associations. It might be that this game of symbols, metaphysical number meanings, phonetic intonations and hieroglyphical codes is one of the origins of gematria in Jewish Kabbalah. Symbolic-allegorical interpretation is also characteristic of ancient Egyptian texts, where material objects are regarded as symbols of the spiritual world.

In the texts of the Third and Fourth Dynasties of Egypt, we can already see a hermeneutic distance that determines the levels of semiotic hierarchy. The name (*ren*) mediates between the actions of a cult ("here") and the domain of sacred meaning and archetypes ("there"). For example, a text that describes the embalming ritual is depicted as a ritualistic drama full of analogies and mythical references. The body of a pharaoh is referred to as Osiris, the performers of the ritual are called by the names of the gods, bodily fluids are referred to as seas and lakes. This earthly play is enacted by an archetypal example, embodied by a corresponding mythical constellation. The body of Osiris is resurrected, and thus, from his seed, Isis gives birth to Horus, the heir to the throne.

Sacred hermeneutics and the names of the gods both possess theurgical powers. A word, if uttered and comprehended correctly, can help one ascend into the world of noetic lights. A transformed soul, which transcends the kingdom of Osiris and steps into the barge of Ra, becomes *Akh*—the higher form of the spirit. This word has a lot of meanings, including

35. Jan Assmann, *Ägypten: Theologie und Frömmigkeit einer frühen Hochkultur*, Priscels, Moscow, 1999, p. 135–136.

to shine and *to glow*, while *akhu* is the source of this glowing, manipulated by liturgy and hermeneutics. *Akhu* is the power characteristic to sacred names and magic words. With its help, transcendental principles appear as immanent and thus can enlighten and sacralise consciousness. The theurgical power of *akhu* belongs to the gods *(neteru)*.

A light-radiating word reveals the sacred meaning of ritualistic actions and texts by explaining the world from the point of view of the domain of *akh* (or the noetic cosmos). The knowledge of Thoth, Ra and Isis possesses *akhu*—the transforming power of sacred light. The liturgical words, uttered during religious rites, also possess this power; thus, they are regarded as "the language of the gods". Magic words *(hekau)* have magical protective power. They even resurrect Osiris—not physically, but spiritually.

In Egyptian culture, every person and object has a secret name. This name is the deep-rooted meaning of a visible phenomenon, the inner reality of an external symbol, or a mask, which can be revealed by the procedure of interpretation. There exists a hidden true meaning, the true name of a phenomenon or an object. It is most likely from here that we get the concept of a hidden meaning *(huponoia)* used in Hellenic hermeneutics.

· THE CONTINUITY OF THE SACRED TRADITION OF
EGYPTIAN PRIESTS ·

The *Teaching for King Merykara*, a literary composition from the Middle Kingdom, lists all the powers of God and states that God knows every name in existence *(Merik. 47)*. A divine name has the ability to create a sacred field, no matter if it is uttered or written down. The symbolic visual aspect of hieroglyphs affect even those who cannot read them, as intellectual and aesthetic contemplation surpasses the "cobweb" of information, weaved by discursive thinking. For example, even though Olympiodorus was not able to accurately read hieroglyphic writing, he still wandered through abandoned temples, contemplating on their ancient drawings and trying to understand the perennial wisdom behind them. Modern researchers often refer to Hermetical treatises on alchemy, astrology and magic as "technical Hermeticism", contrasting it to "philosophical Hermeticism". The Edfu catalogue and the books listed by Clement of Alexandria are classified as "technical Hermeticism".

It might be that there exists a continuity between Thoth's literature and Hermetic literature and that some Hellenic texts, attributed to Hermes, are newly edited translations of Egyptian sources. They are most likely adapted and interpreted taking into account the science of the Greek-Roman era.[36] G. Fowden writes that "It is hardly a secret that a good deal of Egyptian magic really was transliterated, translated or adapted into Greek; and there is much in the Greek magical formulae that can only be explained in terms of Egyptian antecedents".[37]

Oftentimes, the act of translation not only adapted, but also simplified the text for another cultural environment. Mythologically-rich motives and episodes, related to various nuances of Egyptian theology, were usually the first to go, as they were alien to the Greek audience. Even the names were changed, and thus the translation lost the depth created by symbolic phonetical associations. This simplification resulted in the elimination of mythical details and metaphysical allusions.

Demotic and Greek texts are full of references to holy scriptures and the works of the times of legendary pharaohs. This demonstrates the continuity of the tradition of the House of Life. During the times of Hellenism, the nostalgia for the glorified past was especially strong. People looked for examples of culture and spirituality, often projecting contemporary ide-

---

36. Garth Fowden, *The Egyptian Hermes. A Historical Approach to the Late Pagan Mind*, p. 66.
37. *Idem.*

as and topics into the past and adapting traditional mythical models into new historical circumstances. However, the function of the priests of the House of Life remained the same: to manage, preserve and reinterpret ancient heritage. Historical events were recorded and presented in such a way that they would meet the genre requirements of archaic paradigms. The whole semantic cosmos was modelled in accordance with ideal mythical examples; however, the old rituals were also renewed, supplemented and adapted to modern needs. The oracles of the gods could tailor theology and mythology.

Similarly to how the Jews address Moses, the Egyptian scribes of the 1st–3rd century AD address legendary rulers and sages like Tinuphis, Sesonchosis, Petubastis, Setne-Khamwas, Amenophis and Nectanebo. The texts, dedicated to them, are rewritten in the demotic script or in Greek. Sometimes, new material is created in the example of Egyptian works. J. Mertens states that the demotic literature of that time period encompasses all the literary genres of the era of the pharaohs.[38] Ancient mythological texts are also remembered, which is demonstrated by a second-century demotic papyrus about the Eye of Ra, and its translation into Greek. All of this shows that the written Egyptian tradition still existed during the period of the Roman Empire, even if slowly losing its appeal. The last known hieroglyphic inscription was carved in 394 AD in the temple of Isis.

Some of the popular motifs of demotic literature are the loss and rediscovery of sacred books, as well as the role of royal patrons in protecting the caste of knowledge-seeking priests. Both of these motifs came from ancient Egypt. In Late Antiquity, priests and scribes attempted to preserve traditional cults and propagate the wisdom of Thoth, Imhotep and Amenhotep by conveying it in Hellenic terminology.

---

38. Jan Mertens, "Bibliography and Description of Demotic Literary Texts: A Progress Report", in *Life in a Multi-Cultural Society: Egypt from Cambyses to Constantine and Beyond*, ed. Janet Johnson, SAOL 51, Oriental Institute, Chicago, 1992, p. 233–235.

Even though translation of sacred Egyptian texts was considered impossible (Hermeticists were convinced that a text, once translated, lost its theurgical powers), it seems that even the gods themselves urged people to preserve at least a part of the ancient heritage.

After Egyptian temples were closed or destroyed, the same happened to their scriptoriums. However, a part of the scattered priests still performed private religious practices, thus competing with Christian clerics and monks who often held it a virtue to kill an Egyptian priest. By the fourth century, traveling poets, mages and shamans, who represented the weakened Egyptian tradition, were driven out by Christian clergymen, who took over the functions of Egyptian temples and their priests, often using similar worship methods, changing only the external semantics of ritualistic actions. The institution of the House of Life became the scriptorium of the Copts. It is assumed that Coptic monasteries adopted certain ceremonial traditions because some of the former Egyptian priests became the scribes of said monasteries.

Despite different mythology, the religious thought patterns remained very similar. According to D. Frankfurter, Coptic ceremonial traditions and ritualistic texts of the 5th–7th centuries, even if created in a ecclesiastical environment, reflected a lot of topics, methods and tropes of pre-Christian Egyptian culture.[39] The Coptic texts and spells of the seventh century still addressed Osiris, Isis and Horus. People used amulets and talismans similar to the ones used in the Roman Empire. All of this demonstrates that the death of the Egyptian tradition was slow even in a Christian environment. It managed to revive itself by adopting new forms and reshaping old archetypes.

The texts of Hermetic philosophy were created before the spread of Christianity—some of them might date back to the Ptolemaic era or the 1st–3rd centuries AD. To properly depict

---

39. David Frankfurter, *Religion in Roman Egypt. Assimilations and Resistance*, Princeton University Press, Princeton, 1999, p. 241.

the religious and cultural context of Egypt at that time, one must remember that ancient temples were still functioning. Here, all the rites were performed in accordance with the religious canons that dated back thousands of years. Despite Hellenic culture and Greek literature, the majority of the priests were able to read hieroglyphs. They even developed various methods of symbolic interpretation. The elaborate hieroglyphical texts, chiselled onto the walls of the temple of Esna between the reigns of emperor Domitian and emperor Antoninus, prove that Egyptian theology was not only alive, but that it was also progressing and maintaining a stable metaphysical foundation. The architecture of the Ptolemaic and Roman eras was almost identical to the one of the Middle and Late Kingdoms. Before the destruction of temples, Egyptians managed to steadily continue their traditions.

· THE RELATIONSHIP BETWEEN EGYPTIAN THEOLOGY AND HERMETIC COSMOLOGY ·

Egyptians perceived their theocentric universe as a living being—it was a manifestation of the Intellect that emerged from the primordial waters, as well as the cosmic body of the Word of creation. The demiurgic Word is the power of Intellect, which is also referred to as Heart. This Intellect is the source of all the noetic gods, as gods (*neteru*) are regarded as parts of the nonmaterial intellectual body. If the inexpressible depth, from which emerges the archetypal Ogdoad, is the first God (like Numenius' First Intellect or Plotinus' One), then the solar Intellect is the second God, responsible for shaping the noetic cosmos. The manifestations of the noetic cosmos become the manifestations of the physical cosmos. Spiritual world, just like Osiris' Duat, is a transitional state. That is why Neoplatonists localize the Demiurge of the psychosomatic world between 1) a structurally-complicated noetic cosmos and 2) the material world that repeats the paradigms of the former. The Demiurge is akin to the narrow neck of an hour-glass, through which flows the sand of realized potentials. This sand travels from the higher glass bulb of archetypes into the lower bulb of phenomena. The second God is usually referred to as the Son; however, in *Memphis Theology*, this position is dedicated to Atum, whose name means *completeness* or *fullness*. It is the fullness (*pleroma*) of the sacred Intellect that Christianity expresses as the hypostasis of the Son. The body of Atum the creator is the material cosmos, permeated by spiritual vitality. It is a psychosomatic reality with its own hierarchy of being. Atum (or Thoth) is the Heart and Tongue of this reality, or the primordial principle of the hearts and tongues of all living beings. Atum rules all the energies of the noetic and the material cosmos, and that is why the mental and physical activity of everything that is alive directly or indirectly depends on the possibilities given by the Intellect. Invisible gods are akin to the emanations of light, scattered on a noetic level, while visible gods are the crystallizations of this light, dispersed through a demiurgic prism.

In monotheistic terminology, the first noetic god pair, Shu and Tefnut, is referred to as "unborn", i.e. "not created", while the gods of the lower levels of the Great Ennead are referred to as "born". Atum created Shu and Tefnut through masturbation. In a metaphysical sense, Shu is the space of the noetic light, a life-bearing spirit, or "air". Tefnut is depicted as a woman with the head of a lioness, or a cobra, associated with Hathor and Sekhmet. Keeping in mind the mentioned symbolism, E. Iversen notes that Hermetic cosmology emphasizes two elements—air and fire. That is why Tefnut may not represent moisture (as is widely considered) as she might actually represent fire.[40] From a metaphysical point of view, it is a prototype of demiurgic and theurgical fire. While Shu and Tefnut are the "unborn" gods, forming the primordial noetic Ennead together with Atum, Geb (earth) and Nut

---

40. Erik Iversen, *Egyptian and Hermetic Doctrine*, Museum Tusculanum Press, Copenhagen, 1984, p. 13, 11.

(sky) are considered as "born" and thus belong to a lower ontological category.

According to Iamblichus, Egyptians clearly differentiated between the noetic and physical worlds on both cosmic and microcosmic levels. By assuming that the physical realm is not the only plane of existence, Egyptians worshipped pure Intellect (*katharon te noun huper ton kosmon protitheasi—De Myster.* 267.4). According to E. Iversen, the *Shabaka Text* confirms these ideas by paying utmost attention to the sacred Intellect and suggesting that this Intellect directly affects all the mental and physical realities.[41]

It is really so that Ptah manifests the gods by granting them existence. The manifested gods incarnate bodies of their own choice, just like the Greek *eidos* ("form") merges with *hule* ("matter"). Ptah also unfurls the Egyptian landscape, equivalent to his own "visible body"—temples, cities, natural surroundings and cult statues. Rocks, rivers, trees, mountains—all of this is the physically manifested body of the Creator, in other words—an immanent manifestation of the demiurgic Form.

From this Egyptian and Platonic doctrine emerges the Hermetic theory on the sacred origins of material qualities and individual substances. The Intellect, which surpasses the natural and cosmic reality, is the source of the manifestations of the physical world. In this regard, Atum is the intellectual heart of Ptah, whose "thoughts" are expressed by the Word (*Logos*). Hierarchically, Atum's Ennead (whose gods are compared with Atum's lips and teeth that utter the names of all the objects) forms the third level of divinity.

The names of Ptah and Atum can be replaced with other names, preserving the same metaphysical schema: some of the known pairs are Ptah and Ra, Amon and Ra, Khnum and Ra, Ra and Horakhty, Sobek and Ra. There exist lots of other cosmogonical variants that complement each other but are not regarded as dogmas.

---

41. *Ibid.,* p. 16.

The Creator, who emerged from the primordial waters (in the *Memphis Theology*: Ptah-Nun, Ptah), is closely related to the Creator of the material world. The highest Primordial Principle is referred to as "the Only One" (*ua*), "the one who existed before being itself," "the maker of everything, what is and what is not." This Primordial Principle maintains the whole world of manifestations. Just like in Plato's philosophy, earthly phenomena are the reflections of noetic paradigms, as the physical cosmos reflects and extends the noetic cosmos on another ontological level, physically expressing the completeness of the archetypes of Atum and his Ennead. That is why human nature is twofold: the body belongs to the physical realm, while the intellect (or the spirit, *akh*) belongs to the noetic world. In the latter aspect, a human being is not a creation of the Demiurge of the material world, but rather a creation of the Primordial Principle, made in His own image. The *Teaching for King Merykara* reads: "Provide for men, the cattle of God, for he made heaven and earth at their desire. He suppressed the greed of the waters, he gave the breath of life to their noses, for they are likenesses of Him which issued from His flesh." As stated by E. Iversen, it is important to differentiate between the spiritual and physical modes of being because this allows us to better understand Egyptian cosmology, showing that ancient Egyptian theology is the predecessor of the philosophical theory of Ideas.[42]

The Universe, in which this image of God (*tut*) lives, is permeated with the breath of life—*suh en ankh*, which is analogous to the Greek pneuma. The soul (*ba*), which returns to the source of noetic light, completes the snake-like circle of demiurgy and manifestation. The breath of life that flows through the body of the cosmic "snake", in its essence, is the manifestation of the sacred Intellect. Egyptian medical texts explain that *suh en ankh* enters through the nose and then reaches the lungs and the heart, which distribute this pneuma (as well as physical sensations) throughout the whole body.

---

42. *Ibid.*, p. 16.

The breath of life is immanent to being itself. It comes directly from the Creator who, in this case, is called Amon, or Amun—the "hidden", "invisible" deity related to Shu, as well as all the manifestations of life, spirit, air and wind.

Life, given by the Creator, scatters throughout the whole universe just like the air, immanent to all things. Despite the all-permeating life (thanks to which even Plato's cosmos is a living being), there are clear borders between noetic and physical manifestations, emphasizing transitional levels of being and different degrees of the hierarchy of reality.

The Hermetic structure of being is also crowned by an only God, the transcendent Creator of all the existing archetypes and elements, on whom depends the hierarchy of existence. The second God is the noetic cosmos, or the divine light that forms the sacred Intellect (Nous). Through the noetic domain, the powers of the Highest Principle reach the material domain, where the invisible Creator is represented by the visible Sun (Helios, or Ra in the form of a disc). The Sun performs the role of a psychosomatic Demiurge in respect of the eight celestial spheres. These spheres are controlled by daemons, who are responsible for all that is material. A human being is a macrocosm, partially dependent on these daemons; however, a human is able to transcend his fate with the help of his intellect.

These cosmological details (planetary spheres, astrological effect of the daemons) are borrowed from Hellenistic science, which is a speculatory mix of the ideas of the Greeks, Chaldeans and Persians. This was an attempt to keep up with contemporary science that was obsessed with fantastical and symbolic astronomy. However, the metaphysical perspective remains: despite the ontological hierarchy and different levels of consciousness, everything is a part of the same God (or his immanent body). Everything is one (CH XII.8; XIII.17; XVI.3). The world of phenomena changes, but the archetypal completeness is eternal and indestructible. God's power maintains all the components of being and is never exhausted. That is why the hierarchy of cosmic manifestations is characterized by *sympatheia*: the parts of the universe form a logical structure where all the elements of different levels of being are closely connected.

The universe-controlling forces that cannot be empirically explained are personified by daemons, which are mental manifestations of higher divine powers. Even though Hermetic cosmology was partly based on Stoicism, Platonism and Aristotelian science, the doctrines of that time were merely a modernized version of the Egyptian *heka* doctrine. Hermeticists simply adopted these cosmological ideas, which had merged with Babylonian astrology and demonology during the rule of the Assyrians and Persians and were later rationalized and turned into an abstract scientific system by the Hellens.

During the Ptolemaic era, Egyptian priests wrote works on astronomy, which they signed in the name of Thoth, as in the past. They also decorated the walls and ceilings of temples with astronomical images. Egyptian magic was always based on local paradigms originating from ancient Egyptian theology and ritualistic practice. Hermetic magic was built upon the heritage of Egyptian civilization, which, in turn, influenced the whole world of Antiquity.

· THE PARALLELS BETWEEN ANCIENT EGYPT AND HERMETIC PHILOSOPHY (I) ·

After publishing his *Corpus Hermeticum* in 1904, R. Reitzenstein attempted to prove its Egyptian origin, comparing it to the *Shabaka Text*, which was at the centre of attention at that time. However, classicists criticized this idea and thus Reitzenstein changed his opinion, now relating the corpus to the texts of the Persian religion. This hypothesis was quite far from reality; nevertheless, it agreed with the prevailing opinion, which exalted the Indo-Europeans, emphasizing their role in the development of civilization. According to the racist myth that started in the nineteenth century, only Aryans could create philosophy. Any Egyptian or Phoenician influence on the idealized Greek culture had to be denied *a priori*. For example, J. Kroll spread the idea that *Corpus Hermeticum* was based solely on Greek sources and had nothing to do with Egypt. However, it was A. J. Festugière who finally universalized the idea about the Hellenic origin of Hermetic philosophy. Thus, the problems of Hermeticism were discussed only by the specialists of classical philology, who supported the "Indo-European" myth together with the theories of racial superiority. The influence of Platonic philosophy and Stoicism was also approved of, and that is why Persian, Jewish, Christian and Manichean prototypes of *Corpus Hermeticum* were also considered as a possibility.

F. Petrie's efforts to prove the Egyptian origin of the Hermetic texts were in vain because he made a chronological mistake, ascribing these texts to the Achaemenidian period. As a result, he was not taken seriously. B. Stricker and P. Derchain also talked about the possible connection between Egypt and Greek philosophy, as well as the connection between Hermetica and local Egyptian traditions. However, their ideas were also ignored.[43] According to E. Iversen, in order to prove that Hermetic worldview, in its fundamental principles and concepts, is related to the mythical imagery of ancient Egyptian theology (transformed and translated into the Greek philosophical discourse), one needs an approach of an Egyptologist, not an expert on classical philology.[44]

Hermetic philosophy succumbs to both Greek and Egyptian interpretation. *Poimandres*, the first treatise in *Corpus Hermeticum*, describes how darkness turns into water. This description is akin to the cosmogonic Egyptian paradigms that speak about the darkness of the primordial waters. This darkness is the source of hidden potencies. From it, there emerges the light of the Intellect. The mentioned Hermetic text states

---

43. B. Sticker, "The Corpus Hermeticum", *Mnemosyne*, vol.II, 1949, p. 79–90; P. Derchain, "L'authenticité de l'inspiration égyptienne dans le Corpus Hermeticum", *Revue de l'Histoire des Religions*, Annales du Musée Guimet, t. CLXI, 1960.
44. Erik Iversen, *Egyptian and Hermetic Doctrine*, p. 32.

that the demiurgic Word, before entering the natural world, rested in the inexpressible state, which existed even before the separation of Heaven and Earth.

The Hermetic Word, which comes from the Light and is identical to it, is the equivalent of the Egyptian *medu neter*, while the Light is the sacred Intellect (*Nous*, Atum-Ra). Just like the Intellect of the Egyptian cosmogony, *Nous* is also referred to as the Son of God. In this regard, some parts of the concepts of cosmogonies of *Poimandres* reflect the ideas of the cosmogonies of Memphis and Heliopolis. Ouroboros, a symbol so well-liked by the Hermeticists, also stems from the Egyptian culture.

In Hermetic texts, the powers that unite and maintain the cosmic structure are sometimes called "energies" or "lights", and they are said to originate from the stars, the Sun and the planets. (CH XVI.5; *Ascl.* 19). They affect both mortal and immortal bodies. These energies are the reason behind all the bodily sensations, growth and decay in the natural world. Additionally, they rule all kinds of political, social and economic domains, as they are the daemonic sources behind arts and sciences (*SH* IV.6-17). Every natural element, plant, mineral, animal or even a member of the human body has a connection with a different planet, daemon or a sacred primordial principle. One can manipulate this mechanism by knowing its fundamental structure and mastering appropriate magical techniques, like well-timed rituals, formulas that connect different levels of being, or talismans that represent other objects.

Iatromathematics, a science that applies astrology to medicine, is also based on these ideas. As we know, the teachings of cosmic sympathy are closely related to Hermetic astrology and daemonology. Sympathetic energies, cosmic forces (*dunameis*) and the emanations of sacred primordial principles are referred to as daemons, or demons. Incorporeal daemons, whose will belongs to the irrational domain of mental determinations, permeate the bodies of people by trying to control them. In turn, daemonology is based on the doctrine of determinism, which became popular during the times of

142

Hellenism and which was regarded as "based in science". In ancient Egyptian culture, stars are also regarded as archetypes, or the dwellings of souls and spiritual light. However, they do not represent the power of daemonized determinism, as astrological fatalism comes from Hellenized Mesopotamia. Nevertheless, just like the Egyptian *ba* ascends into the sacred light (*akh*), the soul in Hermeticism ascends in order to unite with God.

The "technical" aspects of Hermetic teachings are *propaideia* —the preparation for philosophical mysteries, or contemplation related to the sacred knowledge (*gnosis*). Some forces (*dunameis*) fight against other forces, and that is why life is regarded as a cosmic drama with characters of different ontological levels.

The Hellenic *dunamis* is the equivalent of the Egyptian *sekhem*. The power of Ptah's noetic manifestations is the power of the Heart and Tongue. This power is responsible for the hearts and tongues of all living creatures. The human senses (like sight and hearing), together with breathing, all meet in the heart, which turn all of this into thinking. In turn, the tongue utters the thoughts of the heart.

As if reiterating the teachings of the Shabaka texts, Hermetic philosophy claims that it is God's *logos* that allows a human to hear and see (CH I.6). Both intellectual perception (*noesis*) and sensory perception (*aisthesis*) are based on the manifestations of sacred forces, and that is because the universe is akin to the material body of the Demiurge. In this regard, "the world" is the second God (CH VIII.1), or Atum, who represents the unity of all the levels of being. In addition, Hermeticism emphasizes the sexual binarity of God (CH VIII.1), referring to "the world" as the Son of God. In a metaphysical sense, this "world" is a noetic "world" first and foremost, whose demiurgic reflections form the borders of the material reality.

In Hermeticism, "the first God" is sometimes referred to as the God of the Eternity (*aeternitatis dominus*). According to E. Iversen, it is a literal translation of the Egyptian honorific title *Neb neheh*.[45] This God is known as "Everything", as all the objects that exist are the members (*membra*) of his body. Similarly, Egyptian theology regards all the gods as the body members of the Creator. This same analogy is used to describe the human body because, according to Hermeticism, different daemons rule different parts of the human microcosmos. Various Egyptian texts claim that gods reside in Heaven while their images are seen on Earth. Likewise, in his work *Timaeus*, Plato refers to the cosmos as a living being, a visible god, who is an image (*eikon*) of the noetic Creator or the world of Ideas. Meanwhile, the word *eikon* is an equivalent of the Egyptian term *tut*.

Without a doubt, Hermeticism borrowed some ideas from Plato, however, his philosophy was heavily based on Egyptian concepts, which were regarded as his primary sources by Hermeticists and Platonists alike. Even if the relationship between Egyptian theology and Platonism was coincidental or even fictitious (as claimed by the sympathizers of "pure" Hellenism), the Greeks themselves often emphasized the Egyptian origins of their religion and philosophy.

· THE PARALLELS BETWEEN ANCIENT EGYPT AND
HERMETIC PHILOSOPHY (II) ·

Egyptian theology made a clear distinction between two kinds of people: sages (*rekhu*)—the lovers of wisdom, or philosophers (*meru rekhu*)—and the ignorant (*akhemu*). Likewise, Hermetic literature differentiates between a wise person (*ho ennous anthropos*: *CH* I.21) and an ignorant one (*hoi agnoountes*: *CH* I.20). To claim that the category of "wisdom lovers" is a Greek invention is inaccurate. If the term *philosophia* is coined by Pythagoras, it might be that it is merely a translation of a similar Egyptian word, giving it a new undertone.

---

45. *Ibid.*, p. 32.

However, when philosophy gets separated from mythical theology, alchemy, theurgical mysteries and ascetic practice, thinking that it is fundamentally equivalent to abstract logical discourse, the integral concept of traditional wisdom is destroyed.

In Egyptian culture, "philosophy" is inseparable from religious theology, mythology and liturgy, as its purpose is to serve Thoth and to demonstrate a likeness between a god and one's spiritual primordial principle. In this regard, to "philosophize" is to obey the law of *maat*, to practice ritual purification, to follow dietary restrictions, to contemplate the images and hieroglyphs of gods, to give offerings to "revived" statues and to sing hymns dedicated to gods. Such a life of a philosopher, akin to the life of "a sacred animal" (e.g. Apis, the sacred bull), has to awaken non-discursive noetic insights and to reveal the primordial likeness to a god, thus achieving the ideal of "unity", perceived in a mystical, ethical or semiotic-ritualistic sense, which Plato conveyed through the phrase "becoming like God" (*Theat.* 176b).

All of this is possible (and necessary) because the human being is the pinnacle of creation. He is the image of God, able to reflect the sacred Light, just like the living mirror (*ankh*) reflects archetypal Forms (*eidos*) or the face of God. The mirror of the heart is illuminated by the intellectual rays similarly to how the secret inner hall of a temple is illuminated by the rays of the morning Sun.

As pointed out in *Poimandres*, the essence of an archetypal Human, composed of life and light (*zoe kai phos*), becomes the soul and intellect (*psuche kai nous*) during the cosmogonic transformation. The sacred life of the archetypal Human becomes the human soul, while the light becomes the human intellect (*CH* I.17). The Egyptian equivalents of the living soul and the shining intellect are *ba* and *akh*.

According to Hermeticists, "to live eternally" (*aeizoos*) and "to be eternal" (*aidios*— *CH* VIII.2) are two different things. These two concepts of eternity are reflected by the Egyptian words *neheh* and *djet*. According to E. Iversen (whose opinion slightly differs from J. Assmann's interpretation), *neheh* belongs to the solar domain of Ra, while *djet* belongs to the domain of Osiris. Both these terms might be comparable to the Hellenic *aion* and *chronos*, as *neheh* signifies the limitless cosmic time without a beginning or end, equivalent to the infinite space, while *djet* means the earthly time with a beginning and an end.[46] However, different researchers offer different interpretations, thus making it difficult to give clear-cut definitions to these words.

J. Assmann, for example, treats *neheh* and *djet* as two different categories of time. According to him, *djet* is a "finite time", while *neheh* is "fluctuating time", which can be described as "eternal recurrence". In the form of *ba*, the deceased can "enter" and "leave" the *neheh* time, ruled by the god of the Sun. Meanwhile, in the form of a mummy, the deceased rests the time of *djet*, ruled by Osiris. During the night, the bird of *ba* unites with his mummy, thus confirming the integrity of all the levels of manifestations.[47] In this schema, Ra represents the dynamic demiurgical vector (the rites of constant creation, echoed by the patterns of the day), while Osiris symbolizes theurgical finiteness.

The Hermetic idea that the highest primordial principle simultaneously is (*ta onta*) and is not (*me onta: CH* V.9) closely resembles the Egyptian concept that gods and pharaohs are the rulers of both existing and non-existing things. In the *Pyramid Texts*, a deity "utters" what exists and creates what does not (*PT* 1146). "All that is" (*ntt*) and "all that is not" (*iwtt*) makes Atum complete. In this case, non-being means the state of noetic potency.

The Bremner-Rhind Papyrus explains that Ra, before letting all forms of life emerge from his "mouth", hid the noetic essences of all living beings inside himself as potentials, as rudiments of archetypes. This inert transcendent state is represented by the term *nnj*—the apophatic infinity of Nun, the

46. Erik Iversen, *Egyptian and Hermetic Doctrine*, p. 32.
47. Jan Assmann, *Ägypten: Theologie und Frömmigkeit einer frühen Hochkultur*, Priscels, Moscow, 1999, p. 127.

Father of gods. To "summon" (*dd*) something, to utter the word means the same as to express or to create. To "make" (*irj*) or to "give birth" (*msj*) means to give existence to non-being.

The comparison and juxtaposition of the concepts of *ntt* and *iwtt* show us that Egyptian theologists considered the same questions of being (*on*) and non-being (*me on, me onta*) like the Hellenic thinkers of later times. However, as noted by E. Iversen, Egyptians had a slightly different approach to non-being than Plato and Parmenides, granting it a status of tangible noetic existence.

The Hermetic hierarchy of being is bound by *pneuma* (Egyptian *suh en ankh*). The intellect (*nous*) is "carried" by *logos* (*ocheo*), the latter is "carried" by the soul, which, in turn, is "carried" by *pneuma*. In this regard, both Hermetic philosophy and Neoplatonism regard *pneuma* as the carrier (*ochema*) of the soul. Egyptian culture depicts it as a barge, while the Greek culture portrays it as a cart pulled by horses. However, as a life-giving spirit, *pneuma* permeates all the hierarchies of manifestations. It is even possible to talk about different *pneuma* of intellect, sight, hearing and touch, as this spirit maintains all the different parts of a living organism, linking them to their corresponding macrocosmic regions.

Ancient Egyptian medical texts differentiate between "the breath of life", which enters the human body from the right, and "the breath of death", which enters the body from the left (*Pap.Ebers* 100.3-5). The human being here is akin to the symbol of *djed* or a staff entwined by serpents. He is simultaneously mortal and immortal. Thus, the Orphic and Pythagorean concept of the immortality of the soul was most likely borrowed from Egyptian culture.

Hermeticists also emphasize the immortality of the soul. Just like Egyptians, they differentiate between the soul and the intellect, or *ba* and *akh*. After death, the soul faces judgement (*Ascl.* 28). The judgement and transformation of the soul are described in the *Book of the Dead*. Hermeticists partly follow this tradition. As written in *Asclepius*, if the soul is worthy of salvation, it is allowed to return to the heavens, while sinners must be reincarnated (*Ascl.* 12) or deemed to suffer eternally in the depths of the elements of chaos (*ibid.* 28). From the Hermetic point of view, death does not mean the destruction of the elements that comprise a unit, but rather the dismantling of this unity (*CH* XI.14).

According to ancient Egyptians, this deconstruction, which signifies the physical death, is not a consequence of natural deterioration, but rather a consequence of the workings of sacred streams of life, or gods. The physical death is referred to as "the first death", and thus, even in the Netherworld, there exists the threat of the "the second death", which is reserved to sinners. This death is not identical to destruction; however, Egyptian sources avoid discussing the fate of the condemned soul (who is devoured by Ammit), thus neither confirming nor denying Herodotus' recorded theory of metempsychosis (*Hist.* II.123). In Hermeticism, the condemned soul is either punished by evil daemons, to whom Egyptian texts refer as negative manifestations of gods, or it is condemned to roam in the form of a ghost. Egyptian texts also mention a hell-like place where sinners are tortured with eternal fire.

The god-given life (*ankh*) is one of the most important concepts of the metaphysics, cosmology and anthropology of ancient Egypt. That is why to create a sculpture of a deity means to "give birth" to it and to "revive" it. Sculptures are living images of the gods, they are cult bodies, permeated by sacred manifestations (*bau*) or powers (*sekhemu*). This context allows us to understand the Hermetic statement that humans can "create gods". However, this idea was harshly criticized by Christians, who demonized the majority of the traditions of Antiquity.

There exist even more parallels between the theological doctrines of ancient Egypt and Hermetic philosophy. Some of the ten intellectual powers (*dunameis: CH* XIII.8-9), listed in *Corpus Hermeticum*, have direct Egyptian equivalents. For example, *gnosis theou* is *rekh*, the knowledge of the sacred names. The Greek terms *aletheia* and *dikaiosune* are matched by the Egyptian *maat*, which signifies truth and justice. *Chara* has the equivalent of *aut-ab*, or joy. *Agathon* corresponds to *nefer*—goodness and beauty. *Zoe* matches *ankh*, which means

148

life or the spirit of life. *Phos* is equivalent to *akh*—light, intellect, spirit. All these concepts can be perceived on both divine and human levels. In the first case, these are the aspects of integral sacred nature (as the names and attributes of God, or *sifat* in Islamic theology). In the second case, they are the archetype-reflecting human qualities that draw parallels between human essence and the sacred image of God.

Nevertheless, all these parallels and even individual phrases that have Egyptian equivalents are not proof that Greek treatises of Hermetic philosophy are direct translations from Egyptian to Greek. It is most likely that Hermeticists only partly based their texts on ancient Egyptian sources (especially *Memphite Theology*). In addition, one must remember that any translation from the Egyptian language is only an approximate paraphrasing. If all the mythical concepts and the contemplative visual notions are conveyed through the terms of Hellenic philosophy, such a "translation" becomes a part of the Hellenic philosophy, losing its Egyptian touch.

According to Hermeticists themselves, such texts are impossible to translate because Egyptian words possess a hidden spiritual power (*energeia*) and theurgical qualities. Translation deprives the texts of such qualities. Also, the Greek language distorts Egyptian concepts and obscures their meaning. This inadequacy can be expressed by the term *asapheia* (obscurity). It seems that this concept, also mentioned by Iamblichus, is not a mere myth created by Egyptian priests in order to protect and mystify their wisdom.

It is important to remember that, during the times of Hellenism and the Roman Empire, all the civilized world aimed to speak a single language of science and philosophy, and this language happened to be Greek. That is why any philosophical rhetorics followed Hellenic examples, which became a hermeneutic standard. All the mythologies and theologies had to be translated into a universal *lingua franca*. In this process of translation and reinterpretation, there was at least one good thing from the point of view of the Egyptian culture—Thoth-Hermes was a translator and a hermeneut *par excellence*. That is why such a historical shift of paradigms could not proceed without his blessing. One can say that it was a transformation of the manifestations of Thoth himself. God started to manifest himself in different forms, hiding behind new masks, which did not change his metaphysical essence. Maybe this was how the Egyptians saw this cultural shift, and thus they partly transformed their culture, adapting it to the standards of Hellenic science while still maintaining their ancient tradition of rituals, sacred art and liturgical symbolism.

CHAPTER 3

HERMETIC PHILOSOPHY AND INITIATION

Porphyry refers to the Egyptian Hermes as a "theologist" (*De abst.* II.47.1), while Iamblichus speaks about the anagogical "way of Hermes" (*ten hodon Hermes— De myster.* 267.13). Hermes, the patron god of knowledge and science (*theos ho ton logon hegemon*), is worshipped by priests of various religions, as time and space is irrelevant to the power that provides the knowledge about the metaphysical world. That is why, to paraphrase Iamblichus, our ancestors ascribed to Hermes all their fruits of wisdom by signing their works with his name (*De myster.* 2.1–3).

Iamblichus emphasizes that all the books on Hermeticism, signed with the name of Hermes, are translations from the Egyptian language made by philosophers who adapted them for the philosophical discourse of Hellenism (*ibid.* 265.13–15). He also writes that Egyptian priests are the greatest authorities on theurgy. Hermetic books show to the soul the way of theurgic liberation. As a means of spiritual ascension, theurgy itself is a part of the esoteric Egyptian, Chaldean and Hellenic heritage. However, Damascius proposes a theory that theurgy originates strictly in Egypt (*Vita Isid.* fr.3).

Hermeticists themselves often compared their teachings to sacred mysteries. This knowledge had to be kept secret, as it could only be passed on through initiation. Even though Hermetic philosophy rarely uses the specific terminology of mysteries, Hermeticism and mysteries share common goals:

151

purification, spiritual transformation, rebirth, enlightenment and unity with the gods. Even though G. Fowden writes that mysteries originate from traditional cults while Hermeticism stems from philosophical way of thinking,[1] we have a basis to doubt such a theory. That is because Hermeticism's aspiration to transcend the material world is not the invention of the Hellenic era. For example, even *Pyramid Texts* describe the pharaoh's ascent to Heaven with the aim to unite with the gods and the highest Primordial Principle.

During the first centuries of the Roman Empire, people of various societal backgrounds were interested in the ideals of contemplative philosophy and the possibility (with the help of wisdom, purification, rituals and faith) to restore the primordial god-like human state of the golden age of spirituality. However, unlike Christianity, which popularized the idea of spiritual immortality as well as the archetype of the Son of God, Neoplatonism and Hermeticism were never the religions of the masses. That is because these doctrines propagated wisdom that was difficult to achieve. To eliminate one's foolishness, to cultivate one's intellect and to gain extensive spiritual knowledge—these were long and tedious processes (*paideia*) that contrasted the superficial faith in miracles or salvation (which was guaranteed to everyone who merely belonged to a religious organization and blindly believed in mythical "facts"). *Gnosis* was the privilege (or the burden) of the few.

Late Antiquity's interest in "holy people", who embodied the Platonic ideal of "becoming like God", was sparked by Pythagoras' philosophy, which promoted the synthesis of religious and intellectual life. Pythagoreanism, whose principles of ascesis corresponded with the radical worldview of Christian monks, was not the only school of thought that followed the rules of the "sacred" and "untainted" life, established by the mythical theologies of Egypt, Mesopotamia

---

1. Garth Fowden, *The Egyptian Hermes. A Historical Approach to the Late Pagan Mind*, p. 149.

and India. However, it was Pythagoreanism that became the example of an esoteric community to Egyptian Hermeticists, Jewish saints, Gnostics and Christian ascetics.

In this context, to "philosophize" meant to achieve metaphysical conversion (*metanoia*), to become enlightened or to earn eternal life. As such a spiritual journey is not possible without a teacher (referred to as a "father"), this kind of philosophy is regarded as an initiation. From this perspective, a teacher is not only a guide of intellectual studies, but also a mystagogue who helps transform one's soul and consciousness, thus initiating the ascent toward the Primordial Principle. The written or oral doctrines are just tools for the possibility to behold the secret symbols and epiphanies of the gods (*epopteia*).

The "way of Hermes", mentioned by Iamblichus, is one of such initiation-based institutions, similar to the communities of the Orphics and Pythagoreans. Unlike Christian communities, this institution (despite its covertness) does not have universal dogmas or a strict organisational structure. Any spiritual teacher who taught in the name of Hermes could alter the details and methods of the doctrine according to his own noetic insights and historical circumstances.

Multifaceted and versatile, Hermes' wisdom was composed of a whole spectre of scientific, mythical and theological knowledge. Its spiritual teachers led small groups of students and had to take into consideration the different needs and levels of education of each individual. Thus, some students were taught the very basics (like alchemy and astrology), while others were introduced to the methods of philosophical contemplation that led toward the light of the noetic cosmos. The studies consisted of moral lessons, oral questions and answers, text studies, symbol contemplation, prayers, liturgical chanting and various rites. As there was no single canonized set of doctrines (which did not mean chaos, because all Hermeticists relied on the same metaphysical principles), the approach of each teacher was of great significance. This is how G. Quispel describes the Hermetic society:

The Hermetic believer was initiated into several grades before transcending the sphere of the seven planets and the heaven of the fixed stars (the Ogdoad). Then he would behold the God beyond and experience Himself. It is now completely certain that there existed before and after the beginning of the Christian era in Alexandria a secret society, akin to a Masonic lodge. The members of this group called themselves "brethren", were initiated through a baptism of the Spirit, greeted each other with a sacred kiss, celebrated a sacred meal and read the Hermetic writings as edifying treatises for their spiritual progress.[2]

G. Quispel based his knowledge on the works of Demetrius of Alexandria, who wrote that Egyptian priests sang hymns based on a set of vowels sung in a particular order. As the seven vowels correspond to the seven planets and the seven musical notes, G. Quispel makes a conclusion that the esoteric book of hymns of the Hermeticists of Alexandria was composed of Egyptian hymns translated into Greek, accompanied by Egyptian music.[3]

According to J. P. Mahé, "the most ancient hermetic philosophical writings were collected aphorisms such as the 'Sayings of Agathos Daimon', of which only short fragments have been preserved." Such collections are referred to as "summaries (*kephalaia*) of lectures delivered by Hermes [...] [that] invite the disciple to reconstruct the whole teaching once he has learnt the sentences by heart."[4] Laconic sentences, which summarize various cosmological and ethical doctrines, could be used as a means to develop discursive and intuitive thinking. As stated by J. P. Mahé:

---

2. Gilles Quispel, "Preface", *The Way of Hermes*, Duckworth, London, 1999, p. 10.

3. Gilles Quispel, ed. and trans., *The Asclepius*, Amsterdam, 1996, p. 274.

4. Jean-Pierre Mahé, "Introduction to The Definitions of Hermes Trismegistus to Asclepius", in *The Way of Hermes*, Duckworth, London, 1999, p. 101.

Since Hermetism is not a philosophical system but a spiritual way, the main purpose of hermetic literature is not to set out theoretical teaching but to bring about spiritual progress, to raise the individual from the realm of the material bodies (including his own flesh) made out of the four elements, beyond the intelligence of this visible world, the seven planets of error and the fiery astral gods, much above the eighth or even the ninth sphere, up to the supreme God, who is *Nous* and pure, endless and incorporeal light.[5]

However, to claim that Hermeticism is not a philosophy might be too bold. This would indicate that Hermeticism is merely a collection of aphorisms without a coherent system. Quite the contrary—in actuality, philosophical Hermetica has a clear metaphysical and cosmological structure, as well as a consistent worldview. Its different texts reflect different levels of consciousness, which, in the context of spiritual transformation, are referred to as "stages" or "tiers" (*bathmoi*).

First and foremost, Hermetic dialogues serve a didactic purpose, however, some works are intended for spiritual initiation. The introductory studies of Hermetic teachings emphasize the value of a virtuous life. With the guidance of a spiritual "father", the "son" has to "be reborn"—to become a human that reflects the primordial integrity of the golden age. Only then can he witness the sacred mysteries. Rebirth and initiation are divine actions performed by the gods. In other words, the final transformation of the soul is based on faith and submission to the will of the gods. Nevertheless, a person still possesses free will. This is what J. P. Mahé writes about achieving spiritual enlightenment:

This goal can be reached by successively developing three faculties: knowledge (*gnosis*), reasonable speech (*logos*) and mind (*nous*). Knowledge is basically a spiritual awakening and a conversion. It consists in believing that the supreme

---

5. *Ibid.*, p. 102.

God wants to be known and can indeed be known by those who are worthy of Him. It is gained by paying heed to hermetic preaching and by living piously apart from the crowd. Reasonable speech is a theoretical approach to the structure of the world and the different kinds of beings, from the supreme God down to the lowest corporeal things. It is gained by reading hermetic textbooks such as the *General Lectures* and the *Detailed Lectures* (which are no longer extant), or by following a gradual course of hermetic education. *Nous* is nothing like a faculty of abstract reasoning. It is much akin to intuition or imagination. It equates to sight, inasmuch as it encompasses everything at once, even God's infinite essence. It is both spiritual light and enlightenment. It can be realised by special philosophical disciplines and essentially through mystic initiation.[6]

Thanks to this threefold nature (noetic, mental and physical), the human being is not bound to any single part of the universe. He can transcend time and space. Certain mental activities allow him to visualize the "beginning of time", as well as the state of the soul before birth and after death. As most Hermetic dialogues focus on discursive thinking, they refrain from revealing the hidden meaning behind the text, which surpasses speech (*logos*). Intellectual perception and meditation require silence:

> To *Nous* nothing is incomprehensible, to speech nothing ineffable: when you keep silent, you understand; when you talk, you (just) talk. Since *Nous* conceives speech in silence, only (that) speech (which comes) from silence and *Nous* (is) salvation. (*DH* V.1)

Various practices aim to awaken and to strengthen the inner vision or intellectual contemplation (*theasasthai, theoresai*) that can help to experience the non-created primordial principle.

---

6. *Idem.*

A follower of Hermes, who transcends the physical and mental level of discursive mind, speech and imagination, desires to become immortal and eternal (*Aion*— *CH* XI.19–21). Possessing the potential of immortality, a human can merge with the highest Primordial Principle even while living in this mortal world, becoming a tool of the will of this principle (*DH* IX), or even a god (*DH* VII). Here are a few typical examples of Hermetic texts that talk about this process:

> Everything is visible to one who has Nous; who(ever) thinks of himself in Nous knows himself and who(ever) knows himself knows everything. Everything is within man. (*DH* IX.4)

> You can even become a god if you want, for it is possible! Therefore want and understand and believe and love: then you have become (it)! (*DH* VIII.7)

> Only man (is) a free living (being), only he has the power of good and evil. (*DH* VIII.6)

This "power" is given by the Intellect, which can be perceived as light:

> The exterior (things) are understood by the external (organs): the eye sees the exterior (things), and Nous the interior. The exterior (things) would not exist, if there were not the interior (ones). Wher(ever) Nous (is), there is light; for Nous is light and light (is) Nous. Who(ever) has Nous is enlightened, and who(ever) has not Nous is deprived of light. (*DH* IX.2)

> Every man has a body and a soul, but not every soul has Nous. Consequently, there are two (types of) Nous: the one (is) divine and the other (belongs to) soul. Nevertheless, there are certain men who do not have even that of soul. (*DH* X.6)
> Nous (is) in soul, and nature (is) in the body. Nous (is) the maker of soul, and soul, (the maker) of the body. Nous (is) not in all soul, but nature (is) in all body. (*DH* X.3)

157

Just as the body, without a soul, is a corpse, likewise soul, without Nous, is inert. Once a soul has entered the body, it (soul) will acquire Nous. That which does not acquire (it), goes out such as it had entered. (*DH* IX.5)

Death, if understood, is immortality; if not understood (it is) death. (*DH* X.6).

Just as you went out of the womb, likewise you will go out of this body; just as you will no longer enter the womb, likewise you will no longer enter this material body. Just as, while being in the womb, you did not know the (things which are) in the world, likewise when you are outside the body, you will not know the beings (that are) outside the body. Just as when you have gone out of the womb, you do not remember the (things which are) in the womb, likewise, when you have gone out of the body, you will be still more excellent. (*DH* VI.2)

The present (things) follow close upon the past, and the future (close upon) the present. Just as the body, once it has gained perfection in the womb, goes out, likewise the soul, once it has gained perfection, goes out of the body. For just as a body, if it goes out of the womb (while it is still) imperfect can neither be fed nor grow up, likewise if soul goes out of the body without having gained perfection it is imperfect and lacks a body; but the perfection of soul is the knowledge of the beings. Just as you will behave towards your soul when (it is) in this body, likewise it will behave towards you when it has gone out of the body. (*DH* VI.3)

"The way of Hermes" differs from other ways of spiritual wisdom in its structure and trajectory. Hermetic deification is not public or official, unlike the one of a pharaoh, which strongly relies on the rank in the social pyramid. It is rather a revelation of the primordial human essence, the cultivation of the Intellect and the process of knowing both God and oneself. It encourages one to acknowledge his spiritual likeness to the Son of Ra. This acceptance of one's intrinsic divine nature does not depend on the social-economic status. Quite the contrary—it requires to distance oneself from the material world.

Hermetic initiation offers not only extrinsic knowledge, but also the possibility to be reborn as a god-like being, merging with the powers (*dunameis*) of God. After being purified by knowledge and theurgical ascent, the soul is reborn and becomes "an immortal god" while still residing in its physical body. It is akin to a living sacred statue, permeated by the light of the Intellect. Guiding toward eternity and defying death itself—such is Hermes' way of wisdom.

· HERMETIC KNOWLEDGE AND METAPHYSICAL DUALISM ·

The notion of God is one of the most important topics of Hermetic philosophy. In this respect, Hermeticism is similar to the Jewish-Christian tradition, as Hellenic philosophy rarely discusses this topic. Hermetic teachings state:

> Every man has a notion of God: for if he is a man, he also knows God. Every man, by the very (fact) that he has (got) a notion of God, is a man, for it is not (given) to every man to have (such a) notion. (*DH* IX.1)

This means that it is the notion of God that makes humans human. However, only a Gnostic can become a "human" (i.e. an immortal being, a noetic centre of the universe) in the very essence of the word:

> Wher(ever) man is, also (is) God. God does not appear to anybody but man. Because of man God changes and turns into the form of man. God is man-loving and man is God-loving. There is an affinity between God and man. God listens only to man, and man to God. God is worthy of worship, man is worthy of admiration. God does not appear without man; man is

159

desirable to God and God to man, because desire comes from nowhere, but from man and God. (*DH* IX.6)

Even though Hermetic philosophy emphasizes the contemplation of God's actions in all kinds of areas, the aim of this knowledge does not lie in itself. It is merely a means to reveal divine nature. That is why some Hermetic texts condemn those who take an interest in natural science, mathematics, astronomy and music (*Ascl.* 13–14). The single important thing is pure and sacred philosophy, which allows one to know God. However, we should not attach too much importance to this radical approach, as it does not represent Hermeticism as a whole. It merely reflects one of the many strategies in the process of the multifaceted Hermetic education. A student must overcome different stages of Hermes' way, which contains teachings that may contradict each other.

The Hermetic teachings begin with preparatory exercises (*progymnasmata*). Understanding astrology and astronomy is the first step toward knowing God (*CH* VI). Just like the students of Platonic philosophy, the students of Hermeticism start with simple texts, which reveal only a small part of Hermeticism. Interestingly, the texts intended for a higher level of understanding can not only complement, but also contradict the former knowledge. This is where the problem of inconsistency stems from, even though this divergence of thought might be intentional.

Nevertheless, even *logos* has its limits. Discursive thinking and speech guide toward the threshold of intellectual perception, but do not cross it. Then, it is not *logos* that leads the way, but faith (*pistis*). That is why, according to Hermeticists, to understand means to believe (*to gar noesai esti to pisteusai*), while to not understand means not to believe. Faith is compared to non-discursive knowledge based on noetic intuition. That is the reason why there exist two types of knowledge: *episteme* and *gnosis*. The first one is a consequence of the discursive mind (*logos*), while the other comes from faith. The aim of *episteme* is *gnosis* (*CH* X.9). In the tradition of Platonism, *episteme* is the highest form of scientific knowledge, which signifies the contemplation of principles and Ideas. Even though sensory perception (*aisthesis*) and intellectual perception (*noesis*) are closely related in Hermetic literature, and one must become knowledgeable about the creations of God in order to know God himself, spiritual knowledge (*gnosis*) surpasses the study of natural science. In this case, *gnosis* is the true philosophy. Without it, it is impossible to be a perfect and devout person.

From the point of view of Hermeticism, *episteme* is the knowledge of the ternary structure of being, emphasizing the immanent aspect of divinity. God is comprehended by studying and contemplating his creations, thus experiencing the goodness and beauty of his manifestations (*CH* V.1–8). G. Fowden writes:

> It hardly needs spelling out that anyone who accepted the basic Hermetic teachings about the three spheres of being, God, the World and Man, and their unity through sympathetic interlinking, was committed to a more or less immanentist or monist position. To have denied that God is present in all His works, and that His genius may be glimpsed through their beauties, would have been at least inconsistent. Yet some conception of the transcendence of God (as for example the creator of All rather than Himself the All) can often be found even in the most immanentist treatises; and as he rose in due course from *episteme* towards *gnosis*, the Hermetist was increasingly likely to face the World and Man as of lesser intrinsic interest than God, and to long for knowledge *of* God rather than merely knowledge *about* Him. And in this way there might easily arise a tendency to devalue the World and Man and to undermine their integral relationship with God— in other words to cultivate a philosophy of dualist tendency and to emphasize the transcendent nature of the Divinity. The authors of *CH* VI and *SH* IIA–IIB, for instance, speak of a world in which there is no absolute truth or goodness, and in which knowledge of these things is granted only to a select few. Any good there is on earth is a mere appearance, an absence of excessive evil. 'The World is the *pleroma* of evil,

and God the *pleroma* of goodness.' We, of course, dwellers in the Platonic cavern, call some things good and beautiful, and struggle to increase our store of them; yet we are tragic-comic figures, for we never even dream what the divine goodness and beauty really are.[7]

A. J. Festugière notices both monistic and dualistic tendencies of Hermetic philosophy, emphasizing their differences.[8] However, according to G. Fowden, we should not refer to these two tendencies as different and independent doctrines—instead, we should interpret them on the basis of different levels of ascent.[9] The knowledge, necessary for the initial stages of the spiritual path, is later transcended and invalidated as a sin of superfluous curiosity (*periergia*), which craves knowledge for the sake of knowledge (*Ascl.* 13–14). Thus, to Hermeticists, theoretical thinking is merely *upaya*, talking in Buddhist terms—a supporting tool, a temporarily useful symbol and a mind-training "metaphysical mirage".

· INITIATION, REBIRTH AND GNOSIS ·

At the beginning of the twentieth century, R. Reitzenstein and some other researchers raised the assumption that Hermetic fraternities considered the *Corpus Hermeticum* as their sacred text and thus held it as a basis for their religious dogmas, symbolic rituals and liturgies. On the other hand, E. Kroll and F. Cumont expressed the opposite opinion. According to them, a religious or a philosophical Hermetic community with its own distinct methods and rituals did not even exist,

---

7. Garth Fowden, *The Egyptian Hermes. A Historical Approach to the Late Pagan Mind*, p. 102.

8. A. J. Festugière, *La Révélation d'Hermes Trismégiste*, Les Belles Lettres, Paris.

9. Garth Fowden, *The Egyptian Hermes. A Historical Approach to the Late Pagan Mind*, p. 103.

as the surviving texts contained no details on any theurgical rites, and their doctrines were inconsistent and contradictory. A. J. Festugière agreed with the second opinion, stating that "there is nothing that resembles the sacraments of the Gnostic sects. No confession, communion, consecration, hierarchy of degrees of initiation. The only two classes are those that hear and those that refuse the word."[10] Meanwhile, M. Eliade thought that the *Corpus Hermeticum* and other texts were a proof of "closed groups practicing an initiation", which offered "pure spiritual sacrifices".[11]

H. D. Saffrey refers to the liturgy and hermeneutics of Late Platonism as intellectual worship of God, or *religio mentis*: to read and to discuss Plato's *Parmenides*, to create scientific theology, to practice philosophical virtues, to pray and to perform ritual purification—all of this means to worship the sacred Intellect and the inexpressible One.[12] Symbolic interpretation can also be considered a religious action, a certain hymn to the divine. Revealing the unity and harmony of different traditions and spiritual perspectives (Orphism, Pythagoreanism, Platonism. and the wisdom of ancient Egypt, Phoenicia and Chaldea) can be considered a sacramental obligation.

During the times of the Ptolemaic Kingdom and the Roman Empire, Hermeticists followed certain ritualistic rules. J. Bregman writes: "There are also ritual patterns of behaviour: disciples gather in a sanctuary, they keep the revelations secret, there is a ceremonial *catachesis*, and a mystery ritual of baptism in a *krater*. *CH* IV 36 tells us that in the beginning *theos* filled a *krater* with *nous*. and those who submerge them-

---

10. Jay Bregman, "Synesius, the Hermetica and Gnosis", in *Neoplatonism and Gnosticism*, ed. R. T. Wallis, J. Bregman, SUNY Press, Albany, 1992, p. 93.

11. *Idem.*

12. H. D. Saffrey, "From Iamblichus to Damascius", in *Classical Mediterranean Spirituality. Egyptian, Greek, Roman*, ed. A. H. Armstrong, Routledge and Kegan Paul, London, 1986, p. 253.

selves become 'perfect men.'"[13] This Hermetic ritual is akin to the rites of mysteries. J. Bregman continues:

> Surely the *CH*, with its creative *and* salvific noetic beings (*nous-demiurge; logos; anthropos*) provides the clearest analogue to the Christian myth. The *theios aner*, Heracles, Asclepius and the other *late* Hellenic saviour figures do not "create", and they exist on a much lower level of the *seira* of procession and cannot be said to be at the level of the *logos* or *nous*. They are lower reflections, although still divine.[14]

The Hermetic *Nous* is "life and light" (*zoe kai phos, CH* I.9). Meanwhile, the Hermetic *Anthropos* is analogous to Christ— the second Adam, who rights the wrong of the first Adam. The archetypal Human gets immersed into the material world and thus obscures the mirror of his heart and soul, which is *imago dei*. The material human is merely a reflection of this archetypal human, a clouded *morphe anthropou*, which must be enlightened by *gnosis* and which must ascend toward God— the primordial principle and the source of everything that exists (*CH* IV.10).

God simultaneously has no name and many names, he is nowhere and everywhere. A rebirth-desiring Hermeticist prays to the Primordial Principle, the life-bringing *pneuma*, the Eternity (*Aion*) and Helios (the Egyptian Ra, Intellect or the Sun). As *gnosis* is the source of the sacred light which floods the mind and soul, and this noetic light (*to noeton phos*) is non-material, *gnosis* performs a theurgical and soteriological function. However, to Neoplatonist Synesius, *gnosis* is not the purifying knowledge but rather a philosophical understanding of sacred texts. In other words, it is a hermeneutic category that appeals to the metaphysical meaning of symbols.

The Intellect, which unites God and man, provides the light of *gnosis* to the soul of a Hermeticist. That is why Hermeticists

---

13. Jay Bregman, "Synesius, the Hermetica and Gnosis", p. 94.
14. *Idem.*

worship Intellect as the hypostasis of Thoth-Hermes who, in turn, embodies the archetypal wisdom of the Demiurge. This hypostasis is represented by a spiritual teacher. In *Corpus Hermeticum* (*CH* I), the Intellect, or the highest intellectual power (*ho tes authentias nous*), manifests as Poimandres to the humanized Hermes. In the treatise *The Eighth Reveals The Ninth*, the Hermes-symbolizing spiritual teacher merges with the Intellect. This kind of initiation is equivalent to the revelation of the primordial intellectual identity. First of all, Hermes-teacher explains a subject to his pupil, and then allows him to experience it through the light of the Intellect, and thus to "be reborn".

Hermetic rebirth signifies an internal transition to a new ontological level, defying all the negative effects that come from physical existence. To be reborn means to cease to perceive objects as three-dimensional, and rather see them as archetypal images or the manifestations of the primordial principles. Physical birth imprisons the soul in a body, while spiritual birth liberates it from the clutches of matter, which is subject to the workings of planets and daemons.

This type of rebirth (*palingenesia*) is one of the stages of initiation. Such a metaphysical event requires a lot of preparation: a virtuous life based on obedience, purity and piousness. Here, piousness is regarded as a fundamental state of a philosopher who seeks sacred knowledge. On the one hand, there is an emphasis on abstinence, depicting the body as the prison of the soul (*CH* XIII.7). On the other hand, the importance of sexuality is seen in a positive light, as love is a representation of God's demiurgic actions (*NHC* VI.8.65). In order to return to divinity, it is necessary to conquer one's ignorance and to realize one's true nature, which will lead to knowing God. Knowledge signifies a person's transformation and the revelation of his divinity. It is represented by two stages of initiation: the first one emphasizes knowing yourself, while the other—knowing God (*CH* XIII.7–14; 15–21).

Hermeticists agree with Plato's idea that to know God is a difficult task, and that even the one who has achieved this feat cannot convey this experience through mere words. Initiation is possible only when a student ("son") and a teacher ("father") work as a pair. Even if the teacher has experienced the sacred mysteries before, the student cannot do the same if the teacher does not experience them anew. That is why, during the initiation, the efforts of both the teacher and the student matter equally. Such an intimate relationship is akin to the archaic warrior initiations. It is similar to Plato's concept of a "philosophical duo", which regards philosophy as a practice that leads toward the noetic Idea of Beauty.

Earthly ignorance can be eliminated on the spur of the moment if the student suddenly realizes his divine nature and fully accepts God; however, such enlightenment is very rare. Usually, the process of rebirth lasts a lifetime and takes place only after the death of the physical body. This rebirth is followed by a divine revelation. *NHC* VI.6 and *CH* XIII describe an initiation during which Hermes witnesses a deity that manifests in the form of intellectual light. Hermes merges with this light and, in a way, becomes a part of it. He witnesses the primordial source of all life, which cannot be conveyed through speech:

> Let every creature in the cosmos give ear to this hymn.
> Open, Earth.
> Let the rains pour without restraint.
> Trees, be not shaken.
> I am about to praise the Lord of creation, the All and the One.
> Open heavens;
> Winds, be still.
> Let God's immortal sphere receive my song. (*CH* XIII.17)

The student is also affected by the vision of his teacher. Initially, the effect is second-hand, however, the student eventually becomes a participant of his teacher's vision, witnessing the same revelation seen by Hermes, who is now referred to as "father, eon of eons, divine spirit". Both the student and the teacher witness how the eighth sphere of the universe reveres the one above it.

166

· THE HIERARCHY OF HERMETIC RITES ·

As indicated in *Kore Kosmou* (one of the oldest pieces of Hermetic literature), only deeply virtuous souls who attained a higher level of consciousness can be reborn on Earth as righteous rulers, true philosophers, city founders, lawmakers, herbalists, prophets, musicians, astronomers and priests (*SH* XXIII.42). Empedocles and the members of the Platonic tradition hold similar ideas. In the culture of ancient Egypt, these privileged souls were ritualistically represented by the pharaoh (the son of Ra, the embodiment of Horus, the perfect *Anthropos*, the Theurgist *par excellence*), his relatives and the priests.

Kore Kosmou also states that the religious rites, which reiterate divine primordial principles, were established by Osiris and Isis for the sake of humanity. This sacred couple also built the first temples and trained the first priests-prophets so that philosophy and magic would feed the soul, and so that the art of healing would protect the mortal body of the human being (*SH* XXIII.68). Ancient Egyptians held similar beliefs, stating that it was Ra who gave humans magic as a means of protection. In this regard, "philosophical" and "technical" Hermetica are not two completely opposite concepts—they rather constitute a single, yet multilevel and multifaceted spiritual way.

Both "philosophical" and "technical" texts are referred to as "sacred teachings" (*hieroi logoi*), thus emphasizing their special status. Studying Hermes' wisdom is important; however, it is forbidden to reveal its contents to outsiders lest there be grave consequences (*NHC* VI.6.54, 63). This knowledge can be only conveyed from a teacher to a student. This institution of successors (*diadoche*) maintains a continuous tradition.

The initial stage of Hermes' way can be completed by individual studies of Hermetic works, viewing the process of the analysis and interpretation of philosophical texts as a "mental sacrifice". However, initiation and enlightenment can only be possible under direct involvement of a teacher,

167

or a spiritual father. The ritualistic tools, utilized during the teachings and the initiation, can either be material or nonmaterial. Hermetic alchemical processes have a clear demiurgic example—as God the Creator made the primordial composite of the Soul, he uttered the sacred words and combined the breath of life, the noetic fire and various "unknown substances", thus creating transparent material, visible only to him (*CH* XXIII.14–21).

Just like the authors of magical papyri, Hermeticists consider the repetition of sacred names very important. Usually, these names are mantric sequences of vowels, which must be pronounced in a particular order and intonation, during a particular time of the day or the year, and only after long and tedious purification procedures. With the help of sacred names (*nomina sacra*) and ritualistic formulas, it is possible to summon gods or to redistribute divine powers. Without doubt, these mantric practices stem from the liturgy of ancient Egypt—ritualistic chanting and incantations.

The spiritual way of the Hermeticists, just like Platonic dialectics and Pythagorean number mysticism, leads from the Many to the One, from complexity to simplicity. It encompasses a myriad of ontological and gnoseological stages. Aside from the all-surpassing God-Father, Hermeticists also differentiate between celestial and earthly gods. The statues that contain divine incarnations are referred to as the earthly gods. In *Asclepius* it is stated that just like God creates the celestial gods, the Human Being creates their earthly equivalents—theurgical images, which are revived by the manifestations of the noetic gods. Such an image emits the light of the archetype.

According to Iamblichus, material gods require physical offerings, while non-material gods require non-physical offerings (*De myster.* V.14.218). That is why Asclepius advises to worship statues, as they contain the Ideas of the noetic world. The conversation between Hermes Trismegistus and Asclepius, described in *Asclepius: The Perfect Discourse*, is held inside a temple. After it ends, there comes the time for prayer. Interestingly, the men do not burn any incense during their prayer, as incense should only be used when praying to lower gods, not to the highest deity.

This prayer is dedicated to the setting sun, which, to ancient Egyptians, represents the presence of Atum. Facing the south wind, the worshippers begin their prayer with a statement that no one knows the name of the highest Primordial Principle, thus he should be referred to as "God" and "Father". After the prayer, the participants embrace each other—this action symbolizes Atum's embrace with Shu and Tefnut, which gave them *ka*, the vital force of life. Then, the participants share a meal that must not contain any meat (*Ascl.* 41; *NHC* VI.7.65).

These rituals are akin to the Neoplatonic prayers that worship the Sun. Proclus, for example, talks about the light of the noetic gods. Every day, he dedicates his prayers to the rising Sun. With his eyes closed, he worships the inexpressible One—the source of the noetic light. Similarly, through the worship of the rising Sun (Ra), Egyptian priests relive the events of the primordial cosmogony, which do not even need to be artificially reenacted, as this ritual of rebirth is performed by the gods every day on a cosmic scale.

The secret Hermetic hymn of rebirth, which Hermes discloses to Tat, is yet another prayer with a strong connection to the Sun:

> Be still, O son, hear the harmonious song of praise, the hymn of rebirth, which I had not thought to impart so easily, if you had not reached the very end. For this hymn is not taught but hid in silence. And so, O son, standing under the clear sky, and facing the south wind, at the setting of the sun, bow down; do likewise facing east at sunrise. (*CH* XIII. 16)

This hymn is heard by every living creature, as it venerates God the Creator, who is One and All, *hen kai pan*.

The rising Sun illuminates both the temple and the worshiper. This act symbolizes spiritual enlightenment, as the rays of the noetic Sun fall onto the person's "heart"—the mirror of a pure soul. The enlightenment, experienced during the initiation, occurs within. The warm embrace of the rising Sun is replaced by the embrace between the teacher and his pupil. Thus, there occurs an exchange of light and spiritual power. The light, emanated from the sacred Intellect, permeates Hermes and reaches Tat, creating a kind of triad that carries demiurgic and theurgical meaning.

Even though not much information survived about Hermetic prayers and liturgical rites, we cannot agree with the opinion of W. Scott, who claims that Hermeticism involves no theurgy, rituals or sacraments.[15] Even if God is present everywhere, it does not mean that the highest level of noetic consciousness is available to anyone, as if human beings were nonphysical intellects. There exist various theurgical means to enter the nonmaterial noetic domain, including ritualistic sacrifices of various spiritual levels, for example, creating aretalogies and singing hymns. However, the highest form of worship is silence. Neoplatonist Porphyry states that silence signifies purity and direct contact with the inexpressible One. It is the sacred sacrifice of the philosopher, his silent hymn to the One. However, the hymns dedicated to the noetic gods that stem from the highest God are sung aloud, while the gods of the lowest level of divinity are offered physical sacrifices (*De abst.* II.34).

· THE RITUALS AND ALCHEMY OF THE ASCENT OF THE SOUL ·

A certain text from the *Greek Magical Papyri*—called *Mithras Liturgy*—allows us to glimpse into Hermetic rites and liturgies. It describes a ritual of spiritual initiation, akin to the one of the Hermeticists. The aim of this initiation (which can be classified as a sacred mystery) is the attainment of immortality (*apathanatismos*).

---

15. Walter Scott, "Introduction", *Hermetica. The Ancient Greek and Latin Writings which contain Religious or Philosophic Teachings ascribed to Hermes Trismegistus*, Solos Press, UK, n.d., p. 39.

This theurgical ascent (similar to the one described in the *Chaldaean Oracles*) consists of seven stages, listed by M. W. Meyer as follows:

1) The four elements
2) The lower powers of the air
3) Aion and his powers
4) Helios, the sun
5) The seven Fates
6) The seven Pole-Lords
7) The highest god, portrayed like Mithras[16]

The text itself contains a lot of magical formulae (*voces magicae*) and names like Ararmaches (Egyptian "Harmachis"), Phre (Egyptian "Re"), Semesilam (Hebrew "Eternal Sun") and Iao (Yahweh). There are descriptions of various breathing techniques, amulets and ritualistic-magical recipes.

The beginning of the text addresses *Pronoia* (forethought) and *Psyche* (soul), stating that these initiation rites are revealed by the archangel of Helios-Mithros, and that their aim is to help the worshiper "ascend into heaven as an inquirer and behold the universe." The text implies a certain level of secrecy, as well as a connection between a spiritual father and a spiritual son, i.e. a teacher and a pupil.

A certain text from *Corpus Hermeticum* (*CH* 10.7) also describes similar rites of theurgical ascent, which help a soul undergo a transformation. Likewise, the subject of how the soul (*ba*) transforms into intellect (*akh*) is prevalent in Egyptian mysteries. Ascesis, abstinence and purification are necessary before such ascent. The ritual begins with a prayer (*logos*), which is then followed by ascent, rebirth, revelation and obtainment of wisdom. Here are a few excerpts from *Mithras Liturgy*:

---

16. *The Ancient Mysteries. A Sourcebook. Sacred Texts of the Mystery Religions of the Ancient Mediterranean World*, ed. by Marvin W. Meyer, Harper and Row, San Francisco, 1987, p. 212.

I, born mortal from mortal womb, but transformed by tremendous power and an incorruptible right hand!—and with immortal spirit, the immortal Aion and master of the fiery diadems—I, sanctified through holy consecrations! (519–522)

Draw in breath from the rays, drawing up three times as much as you can, and you will see yourself being lifted up and ascending to the height, so that you seem to be in midair. You will hear nothing either of man or of any other living thing, nor in that hour will you see anything of mortal affairs of earth, but rather you will see all immortal things. For in that day and hour you will see the divine order of the skies: the presiding gods rising into heaven, and others setting. Now the course of the visible gods will appear through the disk of god, my father; and in similar fashion the so-called "pipe", the origin of the ministering wind. For you will see it hanging from the sun's disk like a pipe. You will see the outflow of this object toward the regions westward, boundless as an east wind, if it be assigned to the regions of the East—and the other (viz. the west wind), similarly, toward its own regions. And you will see the gods staring intently at you and rushing at you. So at once put your right finger on your mouth and say:

Silence! Silence! Silence!

Symbol of the living, incorruptible god!

Guard me, Silence, NECHTHEIR THANMELOY!

Then make a long hissing sound, next make a popping sound, and say: PROPROPHEGGE MORIOS PROPHYR PROPHEGGE NEMETHIRE ARPSENTEN PITETMI MEOY ENARTH PHYRKECHO.

PSYRIDARIO TYRE PHILBA.

Then you will see the gods looking graciously upon you and no longer rushing at you, but rather going about in their own

172

order of affairs. So when you see that the world above is clear and circling, and that none of the gods or angels is threatening you, expect to hear a great crash of thunder, so as to shock you. Then say again: Silence! Silence!—the prayer.

I am a star, wandering about with you,

and shining forth out of the deep, OXY O XERTHEYTH.

Immediately after you have said these things the sun's disk will be expanded. And after you have said the second prayer, where there is "Silence! Silence!" and the accompanying words, make a hissing sound twice and a popping sound twice, and immediately you will see many five-pronged stars coming forth from the disk and filling all the air. Then say again:

Silence! Silence!

And when the disk is open, you will see the fireless circle, and the fiery doors shut tight. At once close your eyes and recite the following prayer. (539–585)

After saying a long prayer, the mystagogue pronounces "the immortal names, living and honoured, which never pass into mortal nature and are not declared in articulate speech by human tongue or mortal speech or mortal sound":

EEO OEEO IOO OE EEO EEO OE EO IOO OEEE OEE OOE IE EO OO OE IEO OE OOE IEO OE IEEO EE IO OE IOE OEO EOE OEO OIE OIE EO OI III EOE OYE EOOEE EO EIA AEA EEA EEEE EEE EEE IEO EEO OEEEOE EEO EYO OE EIO EO OE OE EE OOO YIOE.

Say all these things with fire and spirit, until completing the first utterance; then, similarly, begin the second, until you complete the seven immortal gods of the world. When you have said these things, you will hear thundering and shaking in the surrounding realm; and you will likewise feel yourself being agitated. (611–624)

After some more chanting and encounters with various deities, including Helios, the mystagogue witnesses "a god immensely great, having a bright appearance, youthful, golden-haired, with a white tunic and a golden crown and trousers, and holding in his right hand a golden shoulder of a young bull: this is the Bear which moves and turns heaven around, moving upward and downward in accordance with the hour" (696–703). This supreme god "will immediately respond with a revelation" (725) about anything that concerns the mystagogue. Becoming immortal (*apathanatismos*) signifies intellectual rebirth: "that I may be born again in thought [...] and the sacred spirit may breathe in me" (509–510). The mystagogue becomes one with a star, just like a pharaoh's *ba* becomes a star in ancient Egyptian texts.

Many contemporary researchers are reluctant to admit that Hellenic alchemy originates from ancient Egypt and that it can be regarded as a modernized version of the mysteries of Ptah-Sokar-Osiris. By separating "technical" and "philosophical" alchemy, these authors think that "philosophical" alchemy is a Hellenic invention, while "technical" alchemy (like metallurgy and crafts) only partly stems from Egypt. There exists a popular belief that alchemy, in its true, "philosophical" sense, only appeared in the second century BC as a synthesis of Greek, Gnostic and Jewish elements.

At first sight, this conclusion might seem convincing, however, it does have its drawbacks. In their essence, the majority of funerary texts from the Middle and New Kingdom can be classified as "spiritual alchemy". Zosimos of Panopolis and his followers trace alchemy to the tradition of ancient Egypt and associate it with the names of Thoth-Hermes and Imhotep. The latest research by A. Roberts confirms this statement and shows that the stages of alchemical transformation are akin to the stages of the rituals that were performed in some of the ancient Egyptian temples.[17] Hence, the ascent of the soul is equivalent to an alchemical transformation, whose stages are echoed by initiation rituals, liturgy and various forms of sacred architecture.

All these forms of expression follow a cosmological pattern conveyed by symbolic categories, which tell us that life is a journey of the Solar barge through different levels of being.

---

17. Alison Roberts, *My Heart My Mother. Death and Rebirth in Ancient Egypt*, Northgate Publishers, Rottingdean, 2000.

INDEX

Abbasid caliphate, xiv, 54, 64–5
Abel (son of Adam), 56
Abraham, 16, 19, 57; as *hanif*, 65
abstinence, 165, 171
Abu Ma'shar, 60–1, 124
Achaemenid Empire, 1, 21, 54, 60, 141
Adam, 16, 57, 164; Assyrian School and, 57; "Christian historicism" and, 14; Egyptian Adam, 23; Hermes and, 60, 63
Aelius Aristides, 106–7
Aethalides (Hermes' son), 10
Agathodaemon (prophet Seth), 20, 61, 119; Hermes-Thoth-Agathodaemon, 114; as prophet of Sabians, 66, 67, 115; serpent and, 112, 114–15; as spiritual patron and dramatic character in Hermetic literature, 112; as universal Intellect (*Nous*), 115
Aglaophamos, 17
Akhmim, *see* Panopolis
Akkadian Empire, 83
Albertus Magnus, 57
alchemy: alchemical imagination, 39, 40, 41, 50, 52; alchemical rebirth, 105; alchemical "transformation" of external reality, 47; ancient Egypt, 73, 78, 111, 174–5; Arabic Hermeticism, 78, 80; Greek alchemy, 111; Harranian Sabians, 71–2, 115; Hellenic alchemy, 174; Hermes and, 72, 124; *Hermes Mercurius Triplex* and, 22; Hermeticism and, 6, 58, 168;

Imhotep, 174; Islam and, 71–2, 77; Ouroboros, 111; philosopher's stone, 111; rituals and alchemy of the ascent of the soul, 170–5; soul and, 51–2; "spiritual alchemy", 174; Sufism and, 72, 78; "technical"/"philosophical" alchemy division, 174; Thoth-Hermes, 2, 3, 174; universal alchemical symbolism, 6; wisdom books, 125; wisdom chain of, 112
Alciati, Andreas, 37
Alexander the Great, 57, 125
Alexandria (Egypt), 5, 120, 121, 154; Neoplatonism, 74; Peripatetics of Alexandria, 80; School of Alexandria, 5–6, 74–5; *see also* Egypt
al-'Allaf (Mu'tazilite theologian), 77
Amon, 99, 109–10, 119
angelology, 21, 50–1, 80
Anubis, 12, 43, 85, 96
Aphrodite, 9, 86
Apollo, 9, 21, 43, 56, 85; tortoise and dolphin as iconographic hypostases of, 86
Apollodorus: *Chronica*, 16
Apollonius Rhodius: *Argonautica*, 10, 16
Apollonius of Tyana, 42–3, 71, 72
Apuleius, 4, 14
Aquinas, Thomas, St, 34, 56–7
Arabic Hermeticism, 76–81; alchemy, 78, 80; Divine Names and Attributes, 8, 77; Hermes, 73–4,

177

as tool for transcendental knowledge, 45; verbally expressed imagination (*lektike phantasia*), 43; Western alchemists and, 45

Imhotep, 94, 106–9, 133; alchemy, 174; as architect of Djoser's pyramid, 108; Asclepius as, 107, 108, 109, 119, 122–3

immortality, 152, 157, 158, 159; intellectual rebirth and, 174; of the soul, 147–8; spiritual initiation and, 170

Indian traditions, 38, 51, 68, 72, 83, 152–3; Gymnosophists, 3, 57 initiation, 78; *Corpus Hermeticum*, 166; as divine action performed by the gods, 155; enlightenment and, 156, 169; Hermetic deification, 157, 158–9; Hermetic fraternities, xiii, 162–3; Hermetic talismans and, 41; hieroglyphs and, 39; images and imagination, 41, 73, 78; initiation-based institutions, 153; Intellect and, 169–70; preparatory exercises, 160; rebirth and, 165; ritual of spiritual initiation, 170–4; secret knowledge, 167; submission to the will of gods, 155; teacher, spiritual father/student relationship, 153, 155, 165–6, 167–8, 169–70, 171; way of Hermes, 151–9, 160

Intellect/intellect: Agathodaemon as the universal Intellect (*Nous*), 115; cosmic Imagination and, 52; cultivation of the Intellect, 152, 158–9; demiurgic Intellect, 88, 128, 135; divine/sacred Intellect (*Nous*), 23, 42, 43, 46, 79, 88, 96, 99, 100, 119, 127, 136, 137, 139, 142; as emanation from the formless One, 27, 88, 141–2; First Intellect, 135; Heart/heart and, 92, 127, 135, 145; Hermes-Mercury and, 22–3, 119; human intellect, 23, 27, 139, 145; human intellect and

Primordial Principle, 138; impact on all mental and physical realities, 137; initiation and, 169–70; Islamic civilization: sacred Intellect as pen (*qalam*), 89; lotus flower and, 100, 101; Paternal Intellect, 48, 109; Plotinus' triad of One-Intellect-Soul, 38; rebirth and, 164–5, 171; rising Sun and, 96, 169–70; sacred father/guide and, 79, 119; seven liberal arts and, 12; solar Intellect, 28, 90, 94, 101, 102, 115; solar Intellect as the second God, 135–6, 139, 142; soul/intellect distinction, 147; theurgical ascent and, 171; Thoth and, 88, 89, 91; universe/physical world as manifestation of the Intellect, 127, 135, 137; worship of Intellect, 137, 163, 164–5

intellectual contemplation, 156–7
intellectual perception, 143, 156, 160–1

Isis, 16, 85, 88, 105, 119; as daughter of Hermes, 10; religious rites and, 167; wisdom chain of alchemy, 112

Islam/Islamic tradition: alchemy, 71–2, 77; art of gardening, 50–2; astrology, 77; Divine Names and Attributes, 8, 77, 149; grammarians of Basra, 80; grammarians of Kufa, 80; Harranian Sabians and Islamic Arab civilisation, 73–6, 77; Hermes Trismegistus and, 54, 61–2; Hippocratic medicine, 77, 80; imagination and Islamic Arabian-Persian civilization, 45; Ismailism, 45, 48, 49, 69–70, 77; Prophet Muhammad, 65, 66, 74; religious law (*shari'a*), 48; sacred Intellect as pen (*qalam*), 89; Shi'ism, 45, 49, 77; symbolic representation, 48–50; three Hermes, 22, 60–1;

'Sayings of Agathos Daimon', 154
Scott, W., 64, 170
Scribonius, 57–8
Sekhmet (Ptah's wife), 107, 136
Selene, 120
Seleucid Empire, 21
senses, 143; noetic senses, 42–4, 47, 51–2; sensory perception, 53, 143, 161
Serapis (Greek god), 35, 106, 121
serpent, 106; Agathodaemon and, 112, 114–15; cosmic "snake", 138; Khum and, 113–14; Ouroboros, 111, 115, 142; primordial Serpent, 110–11, 114; serpent-headed, 97, 99
Seshat (Egyptian goddess of architecture, knowledge and writing), 104–5
Set, 90–1, 121; Thoth and, 87, 88, 91
Seth (son of Adam), 63, 67, 69
Sethe, K., 110
Shabaka Stone, 98–9, 100, 137, 140, 143
Shamash (Mesopotamian god), 63
silence, iv, 156, 170, 172, 173
Simplicius, 64
Socrates, 71, 121
Solomon, 2, 56, 57
Solon, 70
sophia perennis school, 7
soul, 94, 96; alchemy and, 51–2; archetypal Human and, 145, 164; ascent of, 30, 44, 143, 159, 170–5; *Asclepius* on, 147–8; body and soul, 32, 37, 157; breathing eternally, 91; condemned soul, 148; Hermes as guide of souls, 8, 12, 83–6; image/archetype's impact on the soul, 38; immortality of, 147–8; Nous and, 157–8; Plotinus' triad of One-Intellect-Soul, 38; *pneuma* and, 147; purification of, 103, 159; reincarnation, 147; returning to the source of noetic light, 138; sacred guide of souls/

"Perfect Nature", 79–80; soul/intellect distinction, 147; Soul of the World, 32–3, 47, 52, 53, 107, 111; souls of the dead, 93, 103, 147–8; Thoth as guide and patron of souls, 87, 91–2, 103
Steuco, Agostino: *De perenni Philosophia*, 19
Stobaeus, 4
Stoicism, 10, 27, 39–40, 54; hermeneutics, 129; Hermes and Stoic theology, 117; Hermeticism and, 62, 118; magic and, 32, 33; philosophical Hermetica and, 2; sacred name, 129
Strabo (Greek geographer and philosopher), 127
Stricker, B., 141
Sufism, 21, 39–40, 45; alchemy, 72, 78; Arabic Hermeticism, 77–9; Batiniyya, 73; Harranian Sabians and, 72, 73; mind/spirit contrast, 62; perennial philosophy, 19–20; sacred guide of souls/"Perfect Nature", 79–80; world of autonomous images or similitudes (*ʿālam al-mithāl*), 46; *see also* Islam/Islamic tradition
al-Suhrawardi, Shahab al-Din Yahya ibn Habash, 77–8, 80; chain of wisdom (*silsilah*), 20; Light ontology and angelology, 21; *al-Mutarahat*, 79; perennial philosophy, 19–20; "Perfect Nature", 79; School of Illumination, 20, 77, 78
symbolism/symbols: allegory/image/symbol distinction, 48–9; baboons, 93; cosmology as symbolic model, 25; emblems, 36–7; eternal paradigms and, 127; Harranian Sabians, 30; hieroglyphs, 38; Islamic tradition, 48–50; knots, 93; magic/theurgy and symbols, 26, 28–9, 32, 35; net as the fabric of the universe,

www.ingramcontent.com/pod-product-compliance
Lightning Source LLC
LaVergne TN
LVHW011418080426
835512LV00005B/125